STAR WOMAN AND OTHER SHAWNEE TALES

Retold by

James A. Clifton

UNIVERSITY
PRESS OF
AMERICA

LANHAM • NEW YORK • LONDON

All University Press of America books are produced on acid-free
paper which exceeds the minimum standards set by the National
Historical Publications and Records Commission.

For

Betty Frankenthal

Another Star Woman

ACKNOWLEDGEMENTS

While searching for materials on the Wyandot tribe I accidentally came across the folktales narrated by the Shawnee Prophet and written down by Charles C. Trowbridge. That research was funded by the Cleveland Foundation and by the American Council for Learned Societies. I am grateful to these fine organizations for their support, although this product of their investment is serendipitous.

I thank the Siegfried W. Frankenthal family for endowing a professorship here at the University of Wisconsin--Green Bay, and my colleagues for selecting me for this honor, which certainly helps to promote scholarship and--I hope, creative writing.

Dr. Josephine Harper, Archivist at the State Historical Society of Wisconsin, aided me in locating and evaluating the manuscripts and provided vital additional information. I appreciate the Historical Society's permission to use Charles C. Trowbridge "Miami, Wyandot, and Shawnee Indian Legends," Ms. U.S. IE, 1876. How the manuscript was filed under that title we do not know, for the materials are exclusively Shawnee. Would that Trowbridge's long missing Wyandot manuscripts were there as well.

Peter Stambler, colleague that he is, read the original manuscript for this book with a critical but kindly and poetic eye. Similarly, John Messenger, whose advice and counsel I value more than he may realize, cast his gaze across these pages for evidence of excessive jollification. Neither is responsible for any of my lapses.

The original manuscript was written in the old days, B.C. Subsequently, having modernized, I enlisted several capable and responsive electronic assistants. Thus final manuscript was prepared with the much appreciated help of Tel E. Video III, Mannes M. Tally, and Daisy Writer. The word-processing program employed, appropriately enough for this subject matter, was of course WordStar.

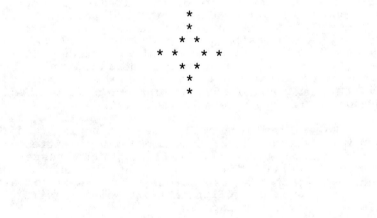

CONTENTS

vii

HALAAKOWI?KWE

The Star Woman

Haa! Katawpi!

--Pay attention! Here is a tale!

Once upon a time there lived a man named **Waapimskwalonya**--the White Hawk. He was a solitary fellow
who lived an isolated life, remote from other **Shaawan-
waki**--other of the Southern People. But he was such a
remarkable hunter that the rafters of his **wiikiwa**--his
long house were generally hung with dry meat.

One season the White Hawk decided to take a
trip. On the first day he traveled ta?pakshimochi--
toward where Sun goes, to the place where he usually
hunted. There he made his camp. After resting that
night, when Sun reappeared behind him he walked even
further onward, farther than he had ever gone before.
On and on he walked until his attention was caught by
a brightness--a brillance that seemed to come from a
distant treeless place. He walked on toward the shin-
ing spot until he found himself in a large prairie.
In the very middle of this grassy place he saw the
ground was perfectly level, the waist-high blue-stem
prairie grasses cleared and cut away, and the clay
soil tromped smoothly down.

As the White Hawk walked over the clearing he
soon realized that someone had prepared this prairie
for playing lacrosse. Indeed, in the center he found
the special hollowed-out spot where the players as-
semble to agree on the rules before starting the game.
And over the whole field he saw innumerable tracks--
footprints, signs of other **lenaweki**--other true people
like himself, he believed. But they were very small
footmarks!

Hoping to find a trail leading from the lacrosse
field to their village, **Waapimskwalonya** scouted around
the outside of the whole prairie. But he could find
no path, not even a few footprints leading to or away
from the lacrosse field. This was a great mystery to

1

him, and he thought, speaking half aloud to himself as a solitary man will do, "I will conceal myself nearby and wait to see if I can discover the answer to this puzzlement." So White Hawk hid amidst some scrub-oak trees near the edge of the field. There he settled down patiently and silently to wait.

Not long afterward he heard a great whirring noise in the air. Startled, when he looked up he saw a tiny black speck at a high altitude, a speck descending rapidly toward the mene?thi--this Island. Whatever it was, its descent was rapid and it seemed to increase in size as it approached. When it came near the tops of the trees, the White Hawk saw that it was a kind of a large shooshooni--a wicker basket and that it contained a dozen people who were seated astride the great basket's rim, swinging their feet to the rhythm of a song.

These people were the Halaakowi?kweki--the Star Women, sometimes called the Twelve Sisters. It was their custom to come every day to play lacrosse on this prairie. While the White Hawk watched them, they arrived on the playing field, decided on the rules, and commenced their game. Inspecting first one, then another, the White Hawk was pleased to see that all of the Twelve Sisters were fair and graceful, but one in particular caught his attention, as she was especially beautiful.

For this Star Woman the White Hawk developed a sudden, violent passion. Unable to control himself, he ran toward the sisters, determined to speak to and touch the one he loved. But the sisters spied him and changed their song, calling back the basket. They quickly seated themselves on it's rim and rose high into the air, singing and swinging their legs, just as they had been doing when they first arrived.

Waapimskwalonya was terribly grieved at this loss. He burned with love . . . at the same time he raged inside with disappointment. So he returned to his hunting camp, and the next morning again crept back to his hiding place, hoping again for another chance to see the sisters. But fearing he might be unsuccessful once more if he went out openly, he killed and skinned a possum, dressing himself in the pelt. In this disguise he once again took his stand in the trees near the playing field.

When the Twelve Sisters again arrived in their great **Shooshooni** and began their lacrosse game, the White Hawk, now dressed as a possum, looking like a possum, waddled as a possum does slowly toward them.

"Oh look there," said one Sister. "that possum is coming to join us. He wants to learn to play lacrosse." But the youngest and the most beautiful-- the object of White Hawk's affection, told her sisters this had to be a mistake. They had never before seen possums on their prairie, and they had best leave as it might mean danger to them. The Sisters soon agreed and so they all quickly got back into their **shooshooni**, began their song, and ascended into the clouds.

The White Hawk was even more vexed by his second failure. And so he hung his head in sorrow as he made his way, almost in despair, back to his camp. So sorrowful was he that he could not eat, not a mouthful, and he passed a sleepless night. But the next morning he was again determined and he made careful plans. First he pulled up an old stump and in it he placed some small creatures he caught--some **kosiki**-- mice. Lugging this stump-full-of -**kosiki**, he made his way back to the lacrosse field. There he changed himself into a **kosi** and jumped in the stump with the other small fellows to wait.

He had hardly done this when again the flying basket with the Twelve Sisters returned. Soon they resumed their game, but while they were playing the youngest and most beautiful sister was startled. There was something odd about the old stump! It had never been on their lacrosse field before! The beautiful one cried out to her sisters, "That stump means us some mischief, we must take care!"

"Oh no!" answered an elder sister, "that stump has always been here. It's full of **kosiki**." So saying she walked over to the stump, giving it a thwack with her **pakwakani**--her lacrosse stick. As she did so a little mouse ran out and the Sisters struck at it with their **pakwakaniki**, killing the tiny creature.

This satisfied the Beautiful One and the game was resumed. But soon the youngest sister again stopped, her attention once again drawn to the stump, now even more alarmed. Again she called on her sisters to

leave the field, but they laughed at her and refused.
To calm their younger sister they once more approached
the stump, again striking it with their lacrosse bats.
It was now that Waapimskwalonya, still shaped like a
kosi, scurried out of the stump and across the lacrosse field with the Twelve Sisters close after in
his tiny tracks. But try as they might, none of the
sisters could strike and kill this little mouse.
Finally, the White Hawk ran up to the youngest sister,
the beautiful one, the one he loved. As he neared
her, he suddenly swelled back into his normal shape
and seized her in his arms. So terrified were the
others that they abandoned their younger sister,
leaped into the basket, and disappeared into the sky,
the youngest Halaakowi?kwe left struggling in the
grasp of White Hawk.

Waapimskwalonya began to caress Star Woman,
speaking softly to her, trying to soothe her fear. He
thought, "I must tell her what kind of a man I am."
And so he told her many fine stories about his life,
bragging on himself, about the abundance of game he
captured, of the happiness she would have if she
consented to live with him. Finally, he promised to
catch a great many ha?thepatiki--raccoons for her.
And at last she was calm, seemingly persuaded to live
with him.

They lived together, Man and Woman, for some
years. During all this time White Hawk remained pow-
erfully attached to Star Woman, anxious to please her
in every way he could. Then, by and by, as happens,
they had a child--a small son.

White Hawk, who swept the clearing in front of
his wiikiwa every day, would leave his young son there
by the longhouse to play while he was off hunting.
One day, while White Hawk was away, Halaakowi?kwe took
the opportunity of his absence to tell her son of her
own life and the circumstances of his birth. The boy
was then four years old, and his mother now told him
that she had decided to return to the stars to see his
aunts and his grandfather and grandmother. When the
boy looked unhappy, Star Woman realized he did not
understand, and so she explained her plans to take him
along on the journey.

The boy said nothing for or against this plan,
and thus his mother busied herself gathering the Black
Ash splints needed to make the special shooshooni for

4

their journey to the stars. She worked constantly at this during her husband's hunting trips, but was careful to hide the basket from him when he returned each evening. When the **shooshooni** was nearly done, Star Woman asked White Hawk to go off and bring in as many racoons as he could kill--she wanted to dry and prepare their meat for winter storage. White Hawk agreed and soon had a large number of **ha?thepatiki** which Star Woman cleaned and butchered, hanging the meat to dry inside the long house, stretching the hides on hoops to cure. At last she had everything prepared for their journey. So she packed up the dry raccoon meat and pelts. Putting these supplies in the basket, she got in with her son, telling him they would fly first to the lacrosse field where his father had first caught her. There they would find the trail to her sister's home. Now she began to sing:

Waapimskwalonya--The White Hawk
Nimaala   --I am going
Nakala   --to leave him
Henoki   --Now
Nakala   --to leave him

Waapimskwalonya, hunting nearby when his wife set out on her trip, heard her singing in the air as she and the boy flew toward the lacrosse ground. Seeing them speeding by in the **shooshooni**, he called out, "Oh my dear wife, please don't leave me without letting me shake my small son's hand."

But **Halaakowi?kwe** paid him no attention. Instead she began singing the special song the Twelve Sisters had used earlier, and so she and the boy rapidly ascended beyond the clouds, toward the Stars.

Watching them disappear, the White Hawk collapsed on the ground and wept, so overcome with grief was he. Later he made his way back to camp, where he roamed around like a **waani**--a man who had lost his soul. He could neither eat nor sleep, and soon he wasted away to bones and sinew. Often he said to himself, "**Niwawiyaakachitehe**--my thinking whirls around." But every morning he tottered back to the lacrosse field. There he would spend the entire day wandering around, praying for his wife and son to return and visit him, his thoughts swirling and twisting around in his head like a cyclone.

5

After a long journey, Star Woman and her son arrived at her father's **hoteewe**--his village amidst the stars, where for some time she lived most happily. But after a while the boy began to grow lonely for his father, speaking often of his fondness for White Hawk and a strong desire to see him. Star Woman tried to smother this longing but she was unsuccessful. Indeed, the son's unhappiness so increased that he became terribly sick and forlorn.

When Grandfather saw this happening he told Star Woman she should take the boy back to the Island to get White Hawk and bring him with them to the star village. Grandfather instructed Star Woman carefully--when she made the journey, in addition to White Hawk, she was to obtain one example of each type of useful game and fur-bearing animal known on the Island of the **Shaawanawa**-- the Southern People, and to bring these samples back to the stars with her, her son, and White Hawk.

So it was one morning, while **Waapimskwalonya** sat weeping by the lacrosse field, once again he heard the same whirring sound from the skies that caught his attention that first day long before. Looking up he could see Star Woman and their son returning, descending rapidly to earth in the great basket. He was overjoyed and welcomed them warmly when they landed.

"My husband," said **Halaakowi?kwe,** "your father-in-law has sent me to visit with you. I am to invite you to join him to live above amidst the stars. He ardently wishes to welcome you. And he wants you to bring with us an example of all the kinds of game and fur-bearing creatures that we had when I lived with you on this Island. My father particularly wishes a **Ha?thepaati**--a raccoon, which I was so fond of."

White Hawk agreed happily. He quickly regained his soul, his strength, his old vigor. He set himself to work industriously, scouring the area around the camp for the different kinds of creatures his father-in-law desired. These would make a fine present for Star Woman's father, he thought. As White Hawk brought his day's catch back to camp, Star Woman dressed each animal, preparing the meat and furs. From each sample she cut off a small piece. These she laid in the **shooshooni** that would take them all back to her father.

6

When they had gathered and prepared what was needed, Star Woman, White Hawk, and their son set out for the return trip. After a long journey, they again arrived at Grandfather's home in the stars. There Waapimskwalonya found a large village filled with people who seemed to look very much like proper lena-weki--True People, except . . . they were all naked!

Grandfather was greatly pleased to see his son-in-law, and they together began taking from the basket the small samples of meat and fur brought from the Island of the Southern People. As Grandfather took each tiny piece of fur, feather, and meat to lay it on the ground, it would suddenly swell into a gigantic pile. Grandfather continued to help his daughter and his son-in-law unload the basket, and when they were finished he called together all the people of his village to exhibit the presents that had been brought for them.

"See before you," he told them, "that my son-in-law has brought for you meat, fur, and feathers of all the kinds known to the Shaawanawa. The meat you may eat, and the furs and the feathers you may use to fashion clothing and to ornament your bodies. It is free to all. Help yourselves."

The people of the stars were overjoyed at this stroke of good fortune and ran up to the many piles of different kinds of meat, furs, and feathers. Some began gorging themselves--others began making new clothing and ornaments. But hardly had they begun to eat and to prepare their costumes when each of the star people was swiftly transformed--their shapes were instantaneously altered. Each suddenly turned into the animal or bird whose flesh, fur, or feathers they had taken from the piles.

As this happened, they all ran off or flew off in great confusion, one as Pshekthi--the Deer, the next as M?kwa--Bear, another as Mhwa--Wolf, one more as Hame?kwa--Beaver, another one as M?thoothwa--Buffalo, yet another as Peelewa--Turkey, a further one as Peeleetha--Hawk, and so on, each of the Star People becoming one of the many animals and birds familiar to the Shaawanawa.

7

And Star Woman, her son, and his father? They
three all took on the shape of **Waapimskwalonyaki**--
White Hawks.   That is what this special name signi-
fies.

Nimechto!

--I have finished!

MESKWANKWATA

The Red-Headed Boy

Haa! Katawpi!

--Hear me! I will speak to you!

     Once long ago there was a large hoteewe--a great village. Indeed, this hoteewe was as big as the towns where live the **Mshimawthiki**--the people of the Big Knives. And this large village had a hokima--a chief, who had one wife and five children--four of them daughters and his youngest child a son.

     Now, that in itself is not strange. Every hoteewe has its hokima, and chiefs usually have wives, daughters, and sons. No, by itself that is not odd. What is surprising is that this hokima, his daughters, even his wife, and especially his son all had **mshkwawiil**--they were all red-haired!

     And this youngest child, **Meskwankwata**--the Red-Headed Boy, was as good looking as he could be. He was tall. He was jaunty. He was robust. He was well shaped. He was so handsome that he had no equal on this Island. And he was near to being a **mayaanileni**-- a New Made Man. But he was terribly timid, this young fellow, more than just modest. He was simply bashful.

     In those days the Southern People, those who called themselves **Shaawanawa**, used to build a sort of platform or shelf along the walls of each wiikiwa-- each long house. Because the **Shaawanawa** did not sleep on the ground, these shelves served them as their **hana?kanaki**--as their beds. And it was up on his own platform, back in the corner of his hana?ka, there under a pile of pelts and blankets, that **Meskwankwata**--this handsome, timorous Red Headed Boy, lay guarding his privacy. There he stayed, day and night, never allowing himself to be seen by any but his parents and his sisters.

     Now, every person in this large hoteewe well knew how comely was this red-headed young fellow.

Especially had the **kwesiki**--the girls, and the **mayawi-niy?kweki**--the New Made Women, the Unmarried Ones paid close attention to rumors of the Red Head's grace and handsomeness. But they never saw him around anywhere. And thus they were very curious. They were drawn to **Meskwankwata**. So much did they desire to see him that they became bold.

And so these young virgins found excuses to visit his **wiikiwa**. Sometimes they went singly, one by one, for one pretense or another. But the Red-Headed Boy took care to remain hidden.

Sometimes these maidens went in groups and were so brazen they would beg his mother to speak to the lad on their behalf. But **Meskwankwata** would not respond to either commands or entreatys from his mother. Even when Elder Sister pleaded with him he would not yield up his privacy, although in all other ways he was the absolute model of obedience.

At last when all the virgins had been often thwarted--individually and as a group, they became vexed. Then it was that they withdrew and made their way to the small **wiikiwa** of an unfortunate woman who lived some distance outside the main **hoteewe**.

This miserable woman had found no husband for herself, for she suffered from a disease that caused her to break out in sores all over her skin. Watching her always scratching these ugly boils, trying frantically to relieve her distress, the visiting maidens called her **Wamaakwakwe**--The Itch Woman. But the aim of their visit was not to help **Wamaakwakwe**. Instead these offended virgins were being hateful, they were looking for a little amusement at her expense following their own defeat. Always they teased her. "Why don't you go to visit the Red-Headed Boy?" they asked. "He will not allow us to see him, but perhaps he will show himself to you."

The young man's four sisters also wanted him to allow the Newly Made Women to see and visit with him, as they wished to arrange a marriage for him. One day Elder Sister crawled up on his bunk and chastised him. "Younger Brother," said she," you are now grown near to manhood! You are of the proper age to marry! I have come to speak with you about this. Your other sisters and I wish you to select a wife from among all these beautiful young women who come daily to visit

10

you. We ourselves are terribly lonely because you never talk even with us. And we would be much pleased if you would get yourself a wife so that we might have both a brother and a sister-in-law to live with us." But the Red-Headed boy would not answer, and Elder Sister climbed down from his hiding place.

After this the young women began to come singly, secretly, thinking to get at the Red Head through his sisters. As each one arrived, Elder Sister would again clamber up on the platform, lift the coverlet from over the handsome red-head, and name the beautiful young woman who had come to visit. She would play up how much each visitor loved **Meskwankwata!** "What a useful wife she would make!"

But to no avail. He always answered with, "You might as well drive her away, I can't let her see me!" And so his sister was again obliged to leave.

After some seasons had passed, the time came when each of the unmarried women in turn had made a private attempt, but all had once again been rebuffed by the Red-Headed Boy. Each of them had been driven away, but none knew the details of the others' experiences. Then one morning they agreed together to hold a council meeting of all marriageable virgins in the village to discuss their experiences and decide what to do. Since the young women soon discovered all had shared the same fate, they began to despair of ever seeing this beautiful red-headed boy.

"Now that we have all been unsuccessful," said one, "let us again go to **Wamaakwakwe,** she who is covered with sores and scabs, she who itches always. We are young and healthy. She is ugly and diseased. But never mind that! We will persuade her to go to the lodge of the red-headed bachelor and try her fortune. And at least we will have some fun out of her failure and rejection."

So they assembled, all the young maidens, and went to the lodge of the Itch Woman. "Well," said one of them to her, "we have all been turned away by this handsome hermit. But we think you may be more successful if you will just try to visit him."

"How can that be," said **Wamaakwakwe,** "When you young and beautiful ones are rejected? Certainly I will meet the same fate."

"Never fear," replied the girl, "nothing risked, nothing won! What you must do is try, and should you fail, we who have failed before you will be your company."

Now it happened even at night the red-headed one never came down from his platform, not even to release his water. For this personal purpose he kept with him on his scaffold a hapkwa--a long hollow cattail reed reaching almost down to the ground. This he used when he had to in the night. Meanwhile, the Itch Woman had decided to wait the boy out in her attempt to see him. And so she made her pallet on the ground just below the boy's platform bed. There she laid herself to sleep--unknowingly, just beneath his hollow reed. During the night she heard a noise. It was Meskwan-kwata, himself stirring around, about to let his waters flow.

To hear better the Itch Woman placed herself exactly beneath the platform, and just below the reed. So it was that, as the Red-Headed Boy found relief, Wamaakwakwe found herself soaked, her hair sodden, her dress soggy and stinking. "Now I know what variety of man he is!" she complained. "Now at last I can go home and forget this whole business. I don't really want to see him, after all!"

"Why should I," she exclaimed, "hoshekita--he's pissed all over me!"

The next morning the young maidens of the village again assembled and walked to the lodge of the Itch Woman to hear of her experiences. "Well," they asked, "did you try your fortune last night?"

"My dear young friends," she replied, "you have made me the butt of your jokes long enough. If you had kind hearts you might have taken pity on me because of my disease, but no. Far from feeling compassion for me, instead I seem to amuse you. No, I did not go to that young man's wiikiwa. Neither did I desire to go. For I am certain if his sisters saw my crusted skin they would be revolted and drive me away. Please, have some mercy on me. Have I not been your laughing stock long enough? Let me have peace in my misery!" The young women, at long last touched with sympathy, agreed among themselves never to pester the Itch Woman again.

Some months later **Wamaakwakwe** discovered her periods had stopped. Her breasts and stomach had grown fuller! She was pregnant! "Alas," said she to herself, "now these young meddlers will have something new to torment me with. They will insist on knowing who the father of this child is. I am embarrassed to admit that I slept under the red-headed one's hollow reed. I am even more ashamed to confess he peed all over me! I can never reveal that. I will refuse to name the father."

A few days later one of the virgins resolved to pay a friendly visit to the Itch Woman. When she arrived she soon saw a great change in the ugly one's appearance, but she said nothing to her. When she returned to the village she quickly told a friend of her surprise discovery; this friend told another; and the next another, until the word had spread to all the young women in the village.

Again they assembled to visit the Itch Woman. "Oh my!" said one, innocently, as they arrived, "how full and round you have grown! What can the reason for this be? You are certainly quite fleshy, you must admit."

"Aha!" said a second one. "Perhaps I can guess a reason for your roundness. There is to be a small one, is there not?"

"Maybe so," responded the Itch Woman, "Maybe so!" and would say no more.

"But how came you to be pregnant?" prodded another, "How did you get this way?"

"You young fool!" responded the Itch Woman. "You ask how I came to carry a child? It is by a man, of course! What other way is there?"

"But which man?" these young innocents asked in chorus. "Name him! Give us his name!"

"Name him now I shall not," the Itch Woman replied strongly. "You will not know the father until after the child is born. Only then will I declare his name to you. Until that time let me be in peace. Nothing you can do will force me to confess the father's name sooner." When they realized how deter-

13

mined the Itch Woman was, the girls departed and left her alone for some months.

Some time later they again collected and visited **Wamaakwakwe**. "Look at you now," said one, "look at how lean you have become! Have you had your child?"

"Indeed I have," said the Itch Woman, "I have indeed. Some months ago, in fact."

"Where is he now?" they asked.

"Dead!"

"Where is he buried?" they demanded.

"In the forest!"

"What did he look like?"

"Exactly like his father!"

"Do you sorrow for the loss of your child?"

"I am greatly grieved, greatly," the Itch Woman replied, hanging her head.

Seeing her apparently mourning her dead infant, the maidens consoled her and departed.

Some time later, during the Days-When-The-First-Frost-Comes, the village virgins once more repeated their visit. This time they found **Wamaakwakwe** busily at work husking **Taami**--corn. "But look," said one, "your breasts are huge! Have you deceived us about the death of your child? You certainly appear to be full of milk from nursing an infant!"

"No," the Itch Woman explained, "I cannot explain how it is, but my breasts have been heavy with milk ever since his birth."

This did not satisfy the maidens, who remained suspicious. Thereupon they resolved to leave, but only to conceal themselves nearby to discover the truth. This they quickly did. Soon they watched the Itch Woman rise and peer intently around, as if to be certain no one was near. She then turned to a large pile of corn husks and uncovered her infant who lay hidden there.

As the Itch Woman lifted the child into her arms, the watching maidens ran up and chastised her for her deception. Looking intently at the child they saw he had bright red hair and realized instantly who the father must be--there was only one red-headed family in all the Island. There was only one red-headed young man who could be the father! And so they clamored and demanded that the Itch Woman admit one fact--that the secretive, unseen red-headed one was the father of her infant.

Now the Itch Woman spoke the truth. "Yes," she agreed, "that handsome, hidden **Meskwankwata** is truly father to my child."

Astonished at what they saw and heard the maidens immediately ran to the longhouse of the red-headed family. There they told the four sisters of the secret they had learned. The sisters in turn related the story to their parents, and the father--astonished at the news, sent Elder Sister to visit Itch Woman to see if all this were true. She soon returned, confirming the report, and father again sent her back with instructions to return with the mother and child, who would live with them.

Wamaakwakwe agreed and set forth, carrying her belongings, with Elder Sister alongside bearing the red-headed infant. As they approached the parent's lodge, Elder Sister ran forward with the small child, displaying him first to her sisters, and then to their mother and father. Convinced that this little red-headed boy was indeed their grandson, the parents happily embraced him and his mother, offering both their love and care.

Elder Sister then took the child up in her arms and crawled onto the platform where her brother still lay hidden from the world. "Look here," said she, "I have a small red-headed nephew. Do you know him?"

"Know him?" said the young man, peering out from beneath the covers. "Know him I do not! Certainly not! Absolutely not! Never, ever have I laid eyes on him before this instant!"

"How can that be?" responded Elder Sister. "Look carefully at him. He has your eyes! He has your nose! He has your mouth! Every feature of your

15

face is copied in his!" But **Meskwankwata** only grunted.

"But he even has your meskwawiil--your red hair! He is yours! He has our **meskwawiil**! He is one of us! You can't refuse him! He is a Red-Head!"

"No! No! No! No!" shouted the angry fellow. "He's not mine! Take him away from me. Somebody has lied to you. I had nothing to do with starting him. All I can remember is . . . almost a year ago I recollect one night using my hollow reed, but I didn't hear the usual trickling sound from below. But that is nothing. Take that red-headed thing away, away from me, away from here! Away I say!"

Elder Sister clambered down from the platform to tell her sisters. When they heard how their brother had rejected their nephew they wept profusely. But after they composed themselves, they advised the eldest to try once more. This time, if their brother would not accept the child as his own, they would adopt and raise him together.

Elder Sister returned to her brother and begged him to confess, to accept the child as his own, telling him if he again denied the infant, his sisters were determined to keep him.

"The child is not mine!" he insisted. "I repeat: send him away, and send his guilty mother as well! I am so miserable over this whole affair I swear I will leave my father's house and never be seen here again! Never! Never! Never! Never again!"

Elder Sister now told **Wamaakwakwe** of their failure and of the red-head's rejection of both the boy and his mother. Full of sorrow, Itch Woman left the village of the red-headed family, carrying her small son in his cradle-board, crooning to him: "Ah my poor child, my small deserted son. Your father is stubborn, resolved to abandon us both. But when he leaves, we will follow close in his tracks."

Before early light the young man made up his pack, hefted it upon his shoulders, and set out toward **wa?shashimochi**--the Place-Whence-Sun-Appears. But soon he discovered that the hated Itch Woman and her infant lived in that direction, and so he turned about and strode off toward **Ta?pakshimochi**--The-Place-Where-

16

Sun-Goes. As soon as **Wamaakwakwe** heard of his departure she took up her child and followed him. That evening, not long after the Red-Headed Boy made camp, she came up to where he was laying.

"Why are you here?" he cried out angrily when he spied her. "What do you want of me? Can't I do anything to get rid of you?"

"Alas that cannot be," she replied softly. "When you left, your small son wept so, I simply had to follow you."

"Well!" he screamed. "You will not have that excuse again! . . . I will end this affair now, once and for all! I will have peace!" Suddenly he seized his **tekhaaka**--his tomahawk, leaped towards the mother and infant, striking each a deadly blow on their foreheads, killing both instantly.

That night, alone and peaceful at last, he slept deeply. When Sun appeared above the rim of the Island, he awoke much refreshed. In high spirits he hoisted his pack, took up his bloody **tekhaaka**, and stepped off again towards the West. But hardly an hour or so after he had departed the cold bodies of **Wamaakwakwe** and her child stirred . . . they breathed . . . they opened their eyes . . . they were reborn!

As the Itch Woman kneeled at a nearby stream to refresh and cleanse herself, she saw her image reflected. To her surprise and delight, no longer was she disfigured with scabs and oozing sores. There was not the slightest trace of the loathsome disease that had long disfigured her. Instead she was fair and beautiful. And her small child had grown rapidly into a handsome boy.

Believing these events foretold good fortune, she dressed herself and her son in their best clothing and once more set out after the father. That night they again came upon his camp.

"Have you come a second time to disturb my repose?" the red-headed one screamed at them.

"How could I otherwise?" responded **Wamaakwakwe** sweetly. "When we awoke this morning our son was so gentle and winsome I was convinced his tears might have some affect on your stony heart."

"His tears do not affect me! His tears do not influence me! I am not swayed by weeping!" he retorted sharply, scowling fiercely at them. "Let me persuade you both . . . once and for all time . . . I will have nothing to do with you!" So saying he snatched up his **pakamaaka**--his war club, and struck the beautiful young mother dead. After gazing down at her lifeless body for some time, he turned to his son and broke his head, slaying him as well. After watching his small butchered body for a while, the Red-Headed murderer rolled the two corpses together and piled brush and logs over them. He then kindled a blazing bonfire and cremated them, leaving nothing but ashes.

That night, again alone and tranquil, he slept a restful sleep. In the morning he inspected the ashes for remains of the mother and child, and he was greatly pleased to find nothing left but a few tiny, charred fragments of bones. These he kicked away into the bushes and thought with satisfaction, speaking to himself, "Now I have done the proper thing to rid myself of those pests forever. My troubles are ended." So saying he lifted his pack and again strode forth on the trail westward.

Not long after he departed, mother and child again rose from the scattered ashes of their funeral pyre, both now more beautiful than ever. **Wamaakwakwe** carefully washed and combed her son's long coppery hair. She purified herself as well, and then, once again, they set forth in their pursuit.

As they walked along in the red-headed killer's footsteps the mother turned to her son, saying: "Today your father will arrive at a village. There he will quickly marry, not just one, but two wives. As we pass by that village it is important for you to present necklaces of wampum to your grandfathers there, and also a fine flock of **pawiithaki**--fat passenger pigeons, that they may make soup for a feast."

When she had finished instructing her son, **Wamaakwakwe** called up to the sky to **Nenem?ki**--to the Great Thunderbird himself. When Thunderbird swooped down and landed before them, she and her son spread their blankets on his back, fashioning a sort of saddle. They then mounted the fabulous creature and flew off towards the village of the Red-Headed Boy.

18

As Nenem?ki soared high above the clouds, Wamaakwakwe turned to her son, saying: "Just as soon as we
arrive near the village I will commence singing, and
we will then fly directly past the wiikiwa where your
father lives. But when we come near we will not fly
high in the clouds. We will plunge close to the
Island so that we may be clearly seen and heard. As
we approach your father's lodge you must spit down on
the ground . . . but your spittle will fall down as
fine wampum beads. Then you must blow strongly four
times, and when you do this four great flocks of
Pawiithaki will fly low for your grandfathers to make
soup of."

In truth, as the Beautiful One had foretold,
Meskwankwata did find his way to this village. And
there he did truly marry not one but two wives.
Indeed, as Wamaakwakwe and her son flew near astride
the Great Thunderbird, the Red-Headed boy was seated
on the floor of his longhouse, between his wives.
These two were employed in doing his beautiful hair,
cleaning it, combing it, parting it, dividing it in
their hands, braiding it, weaving beads and otter fur
strips into the braids.

Meskwankwata, startled, heard from a distance
the swish of great wings and the sound of someone
sweetly singing;

```
Meskwatepeeka--Red Headed One
Meskwatepeeka--Red Headed One
Meskwatepeeka--Red Headed One
Meskwatepeeka--Red Headed One
Nawaatshi     --A son will
A?pwashiwa    --a present
Tako?li       --give to him, the
Meskwatepeeka--Red Headed One
Nawaatshi     --He will
A?pwashiwa    --a present
Tako?li       --give to him, to
Meskwaankwata--the Red Head
Meskwaankwata--the Red Head
```

When Meskwaankwata heard the chant he commanded
his wives to stop braiding his hair--some one was
calling to him! But his wives thought him mistaken
and clutched his braids, fearing he would leave them.

Pulling away he listened closely as the singer came
nearer. Certain he was being called he thrust his
young wives aside and rushed out of his wiikiwa. It
was then he saw Wamaakwakwe and her son astride the
Great Thunderbird--Nenem?ki swooping down just close
enough to this Island for him to stretch up and clutch
at the tail feathers of this amazing creature. But he
could not catch them!

    As they circled and swooped and came toward him,
again he ran to meet them, crying out: "Oh my dearest
wife! Oh my beloved son! How happy I am to see you
again! I knew you were coming--I could feel it in my
bones. Oh dear wife, sweet woman, let me take my
handsome red-headed son into my arms and speak with
him."

    But mother and son flew by without halting or
heeding him. When they came over the village center
the boy leaned over and spat and as his spittle fell
toward earth it became wampum beads of many colors.
Soon the grounds of the village were covered with
piles of beaded belts . . . beaded necklaces . . .
beaded bracelets . . . beaded ear-rings.

    Soon thereafter, looking up, the villagers were
surprised to see four huge flocks of Pawiithaki flying
in, slowly and close to the ground. This multitude of
fat pigeons they set forth to kill with their clubs
and capture in their nets.

    It was then that the two travelers, mother and
son, changed their song. Now they chanted together:

         Meskwatepee --Red Head
         Meskwatepeeka--Red Headed Man
         Meskwankwata --Red Headed Boy
         Meskwatepee --Red Head
         Metha   --You have been
         A?pwashiwa   --a present
         Tako'li   --Given

    All this time Meskwakwata dashed back and forth
on the ground, following beneath mother and son as
they swooped by just over his head. Again and again
he begged them to tarry, if only for a moment. He
pleaded with them to let him speak. But they paid him

                        20

no heed, and went flying low over his head, scarcely beyond his reach.

The mother now sang: "When **Meskwankwata** abandoned his father's village he promised never to return. Never! Never! Never! Never!"

"No!" he called up to them, "Not that! No my dearest wife, I came here only for a brief visit. Please wait for me."

But mother and son ignored these last words and flew off seated on Thunderbird's back, traveling towards the Great Lake. As they passed over him for the very last time all the young man's beautiful red hair fell out and he was transformed into Tiiti--Blue Jay. In this shape he darted after them, beating his wings rapidly, struggling to keep up.

When they came to the Great Lake mother and son leaped into its middle and sank to the bottom. There they instantly became **Waapashaki**--Mussel Shells. When Blue Jay saw this, with great weariness he turned back toward the shore of the lake, barely reaching the beach where he collapsed exhausted on the sand. There he remained for some years staring toward the center of the lake, weeping and sorrowing. At last he decided to dance, to mourn his lost loved ones, and only then did he fly away to other parts.

Now, today, if you catch and look at the face of Tiiti you will find small black marks just beneath Blue Jay's eyes. These are the tears of the Red-Headed one, the solitary one--he who would hide alone beneath his blankets--he who would abandon his son and wife.

Nimechto!

--I have done!

HAMOTALENIWA MANETO

The Cannibal Monster

Haa! Katawpi

--Listen to what I tell you! Learn from what I say!

Once there lived an old woman with her grandson,
a small boy she called Pthe?kawa, which is to say,
Ball. This little fellow was so named because he
possessed a peculiar plaything, an unusual ball he was
always tossing and amusing himself with. Now this
sphere was unique, for sticking out of its side was
one nasty kashkwiipichi--a long, sharp-pointed fang.

Often Pthe?kawa practiced at throwing this odd
one-toothed ball at targets on trees. Again and again
he would pitch it until he could hit his mark every
time. Soon his aim was so perfect he could hit even
tiny birds in flight, while they were darting back and
forth amidst the trees.

Now Old Woman was in the habit each day of going
out in the fields and forests toward where Sun goes.
There she would search out and dig up roots and
tubers. It happens, as you will all know, that there
are two important kinds of roots for eating. One sort
we Shaawanawa call kataapaki--these wild potatoes are
rough outside, tough inside, and bitter on the tongue.
But the other kind, those the Southern People call
ho?ponyeeki--the wild sweet potatoes, are smoothed-
skinned out, crunchy in, and very, very, tasty. Well,
every day after Sun reached the Sky-Center, Old Woman
came back to her lodge, her large bag stuffed full of
these tubers, good tasting and not.

But she gave Ball only the smallest, roughest,
bitter potatoes for his meal. She seemed to be keep-
ing the best of them for herself. It was not proper,
Pthe?kawa thought, especially when his stomach grum-
bled, for Grandmother to treat him so.

Now Ball was a keen, open-eyed lad. He realized
he was getting the worst and the least of the food.

23

He knew each day Grandmother carried home a large bag stuffed full of ho?ponyeeki. He could not believe she ate all of them by herself . . . he did not see her do so. But try as he might, he could not see what the Old Woman did with all the extra sweet potatoes. Where did she conceal them? Who . . . or what . . . was eating them?

So it was one day he made up his mind to watch Grandmother with great care. He was quick to act, Ball was, and that same night, after she told him to get to sleep, instead of crawling up on his sleeping bench he wrapped himself tightly in a bearskin robe and laid himself down beside the fire-pit. But he did not sleep. Instead he lay there wakeful, peering through a small slot he had arranged in the robe. On this first night, as he peeked out, waiting to learn what might happen, he saw the old woman go to a sort of partition in the long house. There she pressed against a peg until a secret door swung wide open, leading into a room Ball had never before seen. Grandmother entered the hidden room, but soon returned, leaving open the door behind her.

In her arms she carried a beautiful bowl which she filled to its brim with the choicest vegetables from the steaming kettle. This magnificent bowl, full of savory ho?ponyeeki, Grandmother now carried back into the concealed room. When she was out of sight, Ball heard the voice of a man speaking softly. He grew very suspicious but he remained hidden from view and lay perfectly still, waiting to find what might happen next. "Soon I will have the answer to this mystery," he thought to himself.

Again Grandmother returned to the fire pit, now ladling into a tiny bowl a small steaming helping of the poorest, scraggiest, bitterest kataapaki. This she set aside on a bench, muttering to herself just loud enough for Ball to catch her words. "There! These will do nicely for Pthe?kawa's breakfast."

The next morning, as was her habit, Grandmother sent Ball out to play. When she had left--to gather potatoes as usual, Pthe?kawa quietly returned to the lodge. Without even thinking of the consequences, he stepped around the fire pit to the special wall and pushed at the peg as he had seen Grandmother do the night before. When the secret door slid open, he moved across the threshold, slipping just inside the

24

hidden room. There on a sleeping bench he saw a man lying.

Surprised at this unexpected visitor, the man rose up and said, "Nilekwal?thehi--Oh my nephew! Why is it that you come in here to disturb me? I must remain hidden here unknown to others, for the Hamotaleniwaki--those Man Eaters are after me. Now you have betrayed my hiding place by opening the door. I can remain safe here no longer, for my special power is spoiled. But now that you're here you may come and sit by me."

Ball entered and joined Hoshi?tha--his Uncle, sitting on the bench. Whereupon the older man spooned from the beautiful bowl to give him some of the tasty sweet ho?poonyeeki. After the hungry lad had eaten his fill, he turned to Uncle and said, "Can you show me how to make a m?tekwa--a bow? And also some some hile-nalwinaki--some arrows?"

"Certainly," replied Uncle," but I cannot go out to gather the needed materials--it would be far to dangerous for me!" He then described the parts he needed, and instructed Ball where to look for the best kinds of materials. When Ball returned with the hickory stave, the white cedar splints, the feathers, and the thongs required, Uncle set to work making the bow and arrows. Ball watched and helped until Uncle was done, then in the afternoon he returned to the other room, closing the secret door behind him, the newly completed bow and arrows in his hands. When the old woman came home she was surprised to see her grandson with his new weapons. She knew he could not have made them himself! Where had he gotten them?

"Why Grandmother," he answered, "today I learned I have an uncle in the lodge . . . He made them for me."

The elder woman was distressed to find the man in the secret room had been exposed. She commanded Ball never to go there again!

"I don't know why you are so alarmed," Ball responded. "Why are you so troubled?"

Grandmother, a frightened expression on her face, described the terrible things the Hamotaleni-waki--the Eaters-Of-Men did. She told Ball how incredibly ugly they were. "These evil spirits are seen only in the shapes of hideous old people and ghastly animals," she told the boy.

Pthe?kawa was not terrified by her words. He was not intimidated by the threat of these dreadful creatures. A bold boy, he replied, "Oh Grandmother, I am eager to see one of these cannibal monsters. Let one Man-Eater just come near and I will shoot my fanged-ball to fight him. My ball will strike him! It will wound him! I know I can hurt him badly! These evil spirits--these **machimaneto** do not frighten me."

When Old Woman left again the following morning in search of potatoes, Ball once more went through the secret door to visit. Seeing that it was fully dark in the hidden room, he begged Uncle to come forth and sit in the open air. "You will be safe there," he said. "I will entertain you by target-shooting with my new bow and arrows, and you can advise me."

The older man was persuaded. For the first time in many months he left the dark, secret, lonely room and entered the light. He spent all morning enjoyably, watching his nephew firing his sharp arrows at a target. And he was pleased to see the boy's skill improve as he mastered the weapon. But after the Sun reached the middle of the sky he became concerned and again retired to his private, concealed apartment.

When Grandmother returned that evening, Pth?kawa told her everything that had happened earlier--How much had he enjoyed visiting with Uncle! But Grandmother was even more alarmed to learn the hidden man had come out of the safety of his room. She wept with fear and implored Ball never again to run such a risk. "We never know when the monstrous cannibal beast may be lurking about, hungry to sink his sharp teeth in some victim," she protested. "Never again play so dangerously!"

But the fearless Ball only sat in Grandmother's lap and smiled up at her: "Never be afraid. If anyone or any thing comes to hurt Uncle, I will protect him-- I will drive him off with my sharp-toothed ball."

The next day the intrepid lad again persuaded Uncle to come out in the light, this time to watch him bring down, with his ball, small birds darting in the trees. And so they again spent the day together, the elder watching with pleasure the younger at play. Again they did not feel danger. They did not see any risk. They did not sense any peril. And so Uncle's confidence grew. Perhaps he might spend part of every day outside the dark, secret room!

But when Grandmother learned of this she trembled with new fear. Nothing that Ball said when he tried to calm and reassure the old woman could make her confident Uncle was safe outside his hidden room.

And so, once again, on the next morning, after Grandmother had departed for her daily labor, Pthe?-kawa led uncle out of the gloomy room, out into the brightness of day. They had been outside for some time, Uncle watching Ball fire arrows at a mark, when Uncle started to congratulate himself for having escaped the hideous Hamotaleniwa. Instantly, even before he had half-shaped this happy idea, both Uncle and Ball heard the fierce growling of a large dog. It was coming from high above them, from the sky.

At once frightened, Uncle cried, "The ugly hungry man-eating monster is coming for me!" Grabbing Ball's arm he hustled him into the longhouse. There the plucky boy quickly closed and barred the outer door. Then, once Uncle was safe in the secret room, he fastened a bar over it, concealing with furs the peg that opened it. Next he swept away all the tracks he and Uncle had made in the lodge. With all his preparations complete, Ball now strolled outside and began to play, innocently, as if nothing had happened.

Suddenly the fearsome Hamotaleniwa Maneto leaped into the clearing, his snarling hound bounding in just behind him. Stomping up to the long house, this revolting cannibal creature demanded of Ball, "Let us in! Let us in!"

Ball noticed immediately that both the evil dog and his foul master had each lost one eye. "What do you wish here, you one-eyed pair?" He demanded too loudly. He was not speaking quietly, with respect.

The ugly old fiend would not answer. Instead he urged his gruesome dog on, who leaped up at the longhouse, snapping and gnashing his filthy fangs, snuffing the ground around the house like a skilled hunter. At last he stopped in front of the barred door, lunging at it furiously, clawing at it with his barbed paws, ripping great splinters from it as he slathered and fumed, trying to enter.

Pthe?kawa quickly reached into his hocheepwipiitaaka--his medicine bag, his sack of special powers. He pulled out his sharp-toothed ball. Taking careful aim he launched it squarely at the savage mongrel. His aim was true! The ball struck the brute just in the center of his head. The sharp-pointed fang stabbing into his skull! The hound was about to fall unconscious when the Man-Eater ran up and seized the ball in both his filthy hands, struggling with it, using all his great strength to pull it from his one-eyed partner's brain.

Pthe?kawa pushed the ugly fellow aside . . . grabbed his ball from his hands . . . with all his skill and muscle pitched it straight at him. While Ball battled with Cannibal-Monster the dog revived and leaped back to claw again at the door. Pthe?kawa now had to pull his ball from the ancient monster's chest to throw it again at the fierce hound. As quickly as Ball turned away, the old man himself jumped at the door, and Ball attacked him once more, again freeing the dog. This back-and-forth fracas went on for many hours until at last the brave boy finally tired from his two-way struggle. Then the monster pair finally broke through the outer door and ran toward the hidden room.

At the inner door the same brawl continued: Ball fought first with the Man-Eater! Then his hound! Then the Cannibal-Monster again! Then the dog! And so on, and on, back and forth. At last the greater strength of the one-eyed pair won out and the hideous old man broke into the secret room. Entering, he approached Uncle and bid him, "Follow me! Now!" The terrified young man did so, showing no sign of resistance. As they left, the One-Eyed man turned and ordered Ball to remain behind. "You are not to follow us!" he screeched.

But Pthe?kawa was exhausted, not beaten. He was not cowed. He refused! No matter what Cannibal Monster threatened, no matter this beast's menace, he would follow close after him!

The injured **Hamotaleniwa,** his wounded cur, and their prisoner had not gone far when they came on a lake. On the shore of the lake was the monster's **kopelekolakee**--his iron canoe. Into this strong bark climbed the cannibal, his dog, and the uncle. As they pushed off from shore, the monster sang out:

> I will devour them all
> them all
> my victims!
> I will cross in my canoe
> my canoe!

He then struck the side of his iron **holakee--** PAK! PAK! PAK! PAK! At this sound the canoe shot swiftly forward across the lake, leaving **Pthe?kawa** behind on shore.

But Ball would not let them escape. Reaching into his medicine pouch, he pulled out his tusked ball and threw it straight at the canoe. Immediately the canoe and all in it were pulled back to shore. Now the Man-Eater leaped from his craft and raged at **Pthe?kawa,** arguing with him. "You must return to your grandmother's lodge," he shrieked. "You will not follow us! You will leave, now! Your uncle will only be visiting friends on the opposite shore. He will return in the morning. I assure you of this, you can believe me."

But Ball urged back: "That's not true! If you leave me alone . . . if Uncle goes without me . . . every time you start across the lake without me . . . if you leave me still here I will launch this sharp-fanged weapon at you and yank you right back again! You must allow me to accompany Uncle to the other shore!"

Tired of all this unexpected defiance, at last the Old Man consented and Ball jumped into the iron **holakee.** Together they crossed the lake, the Cannibal Monster singing as before:

        I shall eat them all
              them all
           my victims!
   I shall cross in my canoe
           my canoe!
     PAK! PAK! PAK! PAK!

     When they came to the other shore, they set out
on foot along the trail leading to the one-eyed old
man's village.

     While they were on the trail, from time to time
Ball noticed flying alongside him a **maachika?potha**--a
wren. He soon realized that Wren was always there,
constantly, no matter which turn they took. Getting
annoyed, he reached into his medicine pouch and pulled
out his toothed-ball, thinking to impale this tiny
bird. Ball was not being patient. He did not understand. He did not see that Wren was his **hopawaaka**--his
special guardian.

     Maachika?potha knew this. Wren saw the threat.
This extraordinary little bird called out to him,
"That would be a foolish thing to do. Indeed, terribly foolish! It is stupid even to think of killing me
when I have come to aid you, to give you favors--
skills and strength to match your boldness."

     "What good do you intend me? What gifts can a
small one such as you give me?" replied Ball.

     "Be patient . . . be understanding," called
Wren. "Be calm. Think! Control yourself . . .
Reflect on what can happen. You must realize Uncle
will die unless you can save him. This old man-eater
lives some distance ahead with his ugly one-eyed wife
and this ugly one-eyed mutt. All of them are in the
same business--they all travel about catching humans,
and when they capture their victims they carry them
back to their village. There One-Eyed Old Man or One-
Eyed Old Woman order them to do some impossible task.
And they threaten these poor prisoners--if they do not
succeed in these tasks, the Old Ones will clap them in
prison and starve them to death. Then will the slav-
ering Old Ones devour them--flesh, sinew, and blood,
leaving only a pile of gnawed bones."

     "That is what this Ugly One plans for Uncle,"

Wren explained to Ball. "That will be his fate, unless you are patient, unless you can find some way to save him. The Old Ones--ugly man, ugly woman, even ugly mongrel--may tell Uncle to kill a bear in a place where bears are never seen. When he fails, he will then be starved, and when he is almost dead, he will be food for the hunger of this loathsome trio. When you arrive you will soon see many other prisoners already there, those who have already failed. These are now no more than skin and bones. Soon they will be butchered and thrown into the kettle."

"By yourself you cannot save Uncle," Wren explained to Ball. "It will be impossible for you by yourself. I know your fanged-ball has great power. But you cannot kill these monsters by yourself, for their hearts are not in their own bodies. Their hearts are kept and guarded in the lodge of Machikeekakashkiche--He with the Wrinkled Shell . . . the Celebrated One . . . the Great Turtle, himself. And Great Turtle lives in a far distant place, at the bottom of Kchikami--the Great Lake."

"Well, then," reasoned Ball, thinking but not speaking aloud, "I will myself go to this lake of Machikeekakashkiche and visit with the Great One. I will speak to the Great Turtle and capture the hearts of these devils by myself."

"That you cannot do by yourself!"

"Why not?"

"Have patience, Boy-With-A-Ball," advised Wren, "have patience and remember you cannot fly."

"Oh yes! I can fly! Yes, I can fly!" cried the brash Ball. And Wren, seeing his impatience, remained silent at last.

When the one-eyed pair--followed by Uncle, followed by Ball, followed some ways behind by Wren--at last arrived at the monster's village, they were met by the ugly, old one-eyed wife. Casting her one-left-eye over Ball, inspecting him, she turned to her husband and snapped, "Why have you brought me such an ugly, filthy, skinny, unappetizing little creature as this, I ask you?" Her monster husband hung his head and made no reply.

But Ball stared up at her boldly and demanded, "Why do you speak that way? What have you to complain about? You three are the ugliest trio that I have ever set my eyes on. Just look at you--repulsive old man, dirty dog, filthy old woman, all one eyed! All with just one left eye. Who are you to babble on about how others appear?"

The Cannibal Monster, tired of all this chatter, told his wife to let the boy be for the time: he was not what he seemed to be, not simply a puny bedraggled fellow. But this lad's turn would come! He would get what he deserved! He would make fine bones! Small sweet bones!

The next morning the ancient one told Uncle he must go out and kill a m?kwa--a bear, for breakfast. "It's an easy task. . . there are plenty of fat m?kwaki hereabouts."

But just as Uncle was leaving Ball whispered to him, "Take care! It is a trick! There are very few bears at all in all this country. But if you conceal yourself and let me go in your stead, I know how to find a m?kwaki and will kill and bring one in."

Uncle agreed and the boy then went some ways from the cannibal village, walking on until he found an old rotted Sugar Maple stump. When he kicked it over a large m?kwa leaped out. Ball chased the bear, driving it back toward the village where he called out, "Pwakeekwa! Pwakeekwa!--Blind Man! Blind Man! Come out and kill this plump bear!"

This blind old fellow did run out with his spear and club, killing the bear. Blind Man then set to work gutting and skinning the huge beast. While he was working Ball stole silently up, slipping a tiny bit of bear fat from Blind Man's skinning knife, hiding it away in his medicine pouch. After it was cut into strips and chunks, all the bear's meat was thrown into a large kettle and cooked. It made just one breakfast only, for the One-Eyed Man, his One-Eyed Wife, and their ugly One-Eyed Dog!

When this cannibal threesome were through gobbling, young Pthe?kawa asked, "May I borrow your kettle? I wish to cook some food."

32

"Have my kettle you may, for a while at least," answered the one eyed crone. "But what you have to cook I do not know. You arrived here empty-handed, and empty your belly will stay!"

Ball lugged the heavy kettle off aways and hung it from forked poles. He built a small fire beneath it. He poured a little water into it. And when the pot steamed, he took from his **hocheepwipiitaaka** the small scrap of bear-fat, dropping it into the simmering water. As the kettle boiled and frothed the bear-fat swelled, soon filling the whole great kettle with a savory stew. This Ball carried to the prisoners--all of them famished and gaunt. "Here is your breakfast," he said politely. "Eat until you are full, please. Take your strength and courage from this fine, rich, tasty bear-stew."

Next day Uncle and Ball again went out hunting as ordered. Once more Uncle hid himself and **Pthe?kawa** was off alone. A second time he drove back a fat bear that was skinned, butchered, boiled--then devoured by the Cannibal trio. Again he borrowed the empty kettle, and one more time he brewed rich, thick stew. Another fine breakfast was eaten by the prisoners, no longer as lean and weakened as the day before.

When breakfast was done and the empty kettle returned to the cannibal hag, Ball turned to Uncle and said, "I think a walk would do me good. I shall return shortly." Soon after Ball left the village he again met friend Wren--**Maachika?potha**, himself. Ball then called for **Waapethi**--for Crane to come join him, and soon this long-legged bird flapped close by.

Pthe?kawa then spoke with Wren: "Now I am ready to fly with you to the Kchikami--to the Great Lake where we can find the hearts of this Cannibal-Monster, his repulsive wife, and that foul hound."

Wren replied, "I, too, am prepared to go."

Crane agreed to carry Ball; the boy mounted his back; and off Wren, **Waapethi**, and Ball flew toward the lake of the Great Turtle. When they reached a certain spot near the middle of this inland sea Wren looped and turned, making a signal to stop. As the birds hovered just above the surface of the water, Ball dove down deep beneath the waves, descending swiftly to the lake's bottom. There he spotted the huge Great Turtle resting in the mud.

"Swim quickly upwards!" Ball commanded Great Turtle. The turtle flipped his way up, and where he had lain, in his nest, Ball spied a pile of hotehali--three hearts attached one to the other. Taking the hotehali in his arms Ball floated up to the air.

Seeing him bob to the surface, Wren swooped down and called, "When you are ready to kill the cannibal monsters you must thrust a large shawpo?neeka--a bone-needle into all three hearts, impaling them, spearing them together! Only then will these three vile monstrosities die at last!" Ball slipped the hearts into his medicine pouch, mounted Crane, and now the three companions flew back toward the cannibal village.

During their long return trip Ball amused himself by squeezing and twisting the hearts. Each time he would pinch one heart the One-Eyed Man would scream in pain. Every time he crushed the second heart the One-Eyed Woman would moan in agony. And when he twisted the third, the One-Eyed Dog would collapse on the ground in torment. At length all three were helpless, moaning and groaning horribly.

As the three companions flew near the cannibal village, Ball at last reached deep into his medicine bag, drawing out a shawpo?neeka--a long, sharp bone awl. First probing and prodding each one with its spiky point, at last he thrust deep through all three hearts, skewering them fast together.

Immediately the one-eyed threesome fell silent. They no longer squirmed or groaned. They no longer breathed. They were at last all dead! Oh! They made ugly bones!

As they flew over the village Ball saw below him the three repulsive, one-eyed, lifeless carcasses. He and his helpers landed, and Ball set to work collecting a pile of dry wood which he heaped over the dead bodies. This funeral pyre he now set ablaze, and only when the flames were roaring did he turn away.

Ball now gathered materials for a huge sweathouse. This he constructed on the shores of the Lake of the Great Turtle. And now he commanded all the former prisoners of the cannibal village: "Gather together all the poor bones of those who have been murdered and eaten! Carry them with respect to my sweat-house and place them lovingly inside! This done, you survivors will join your relatives and friends in my sweat-house! Await me there!"

While those who had been rescued set to work, Ball drew a stone-headed axe from his medicine pouch and began chopping down a huge Walnut tree that leaned over the medicine-house. When they heard the blows of his stone-axe, those inside became frightened and cried out: "What is happening to us? What must we do to be safe at last!"

Ball called back: "All you living ones! All you breathing ones! All of you stirring in there! Get out of the sweat-house! Run to the cool waters of the lake and dive in!" All inside immediately rushed outside. More ran out than had walked in. A great many bounded out as whole living men, women, and children who had been borne in as gnawed bones. Every one of the murdered-ones had been restored to life, cleansed and purified in the sweat-house. All of them together leaped into the refreshing waters of the **Kchikami**.

When they came to the surface, no longer fearful, but freshened and vigorous, they all swam back to shore. Most but not all remembered their former homes and villages. These Ball instructed to make their way back to their kinfolk and friends. But some had been dead so long they had no memory whatever of former times. These gathered together and approached Ball, saying to him: "**Pthe?kawa**, our Elder Brother, let us join you and form our own village together. Let us make our own **M?shooma**--our clan together." These new companions and kinfolk Ball gathered around him, leading them and Uncle back to Grandmother's lodge, where they lived together with great happiness for many years.

Nimechto!

--The tale is complete!

PAKILAWA

Thrown Away

Haa! Katawpi!

--Listen! I am telling a story!

    Kapotwawa--Some time ago. Indeed, a very long time ago, but after The Finisher--Kchimaneto had made this Island, and after Kchimaneto finished making the Southern People. A long while ago, in the time when the Shaawanwa were still in the habit always of wandering around from place to place. Kapotwawa--some time ago it came about that at last the Southern People had walked to the far rim of this Mene?thi--our Island. They had finally arrived next to the place where Sun appears, and they could go no farther. So there they made there villages and there they tried to live . . . but it was hard.

    In those days the Hokima of one large village was called Peyatakoothamo--The Rising Sun, and an important chief he was. But the Rising Sun had become much dissatisfied with his youngest son. So unhappy was he with the boy that he decided to get rid of him.

    One day Peyatakoothamo, this great chief, called the elders together in council and spoke to them. "Because the days of the frost have come," he explained to them, "because there is little to eat here we must again prepare to move our village. All must do their part, and each must contribute. As for me, I will leave my youngest son behind when we move."

    The Rising Sun then carefully instructed his people--when they departed they must leave nothing at all for this small boy--Pakilawa--the Abandoned-One, or Thrown Away as he was called. No food, no fire, not even an ember must be left to warm Pakilawa in the frozen days ahead. That way it would be quicker and easier for the boy, this upstanding hokima explained. "Now, all of you," Peyatakoothamo insisted, "each one of you must carefully put out your fires."

But one of Pakilawa's sisters could not accept
this. She saw the boy was to be left naked and pov-
erty-stricken. She knew he would freeze and starve.
Thrown Away could not survive! He would die! So she
resolved to deceive her father and her relatives. For
this purpose sister stole a small fire-brand. When no
one was watching she carried it to a hole in the
ground where her mother dressed deer-skins. There she
placed the tiny flame, carefully covering it with some
clay.

Soon after there was a great bustle as the chief
and his people prepared to depart. The villagers
placed all there belongings in packs, and when the
Rising Sun gave the signal all poured water on their
fires. Only then did they depart. But as Sister was
about to leave she whispered to her brother of what
she had done, instructing him he must take great care
of that one hot coal because his own life depended on
it.

When all were gone the abandoned boy carefully
uncovered his fire, now only a tiny smoldering ember.
Pakilawa next gathered small twigs and dried leaves
before breathing gently on his glowing spark, blowing
it back into a blaze. Only when he was certain that
his small fire would not go out could the deserted
hungry boy search the village for some morsels of
food, and he was famished before he at last found a
few ears of corn. These he carried to his fire and
roasted for his first meal alone.

On one of his next tours around the village
Thrown Away heard something moaning and whimpering.
"I am not alone!" he exclaimed aloud, thinking he
really did have some company. Listening carefully, he
finally made his way to the wiikiwa where he heard the
whining sounds. There he discovered that one of the
villagers had left behind a Chakiwi?shi--one of the
village pups, a tiny scrawny creature, himself almost
frozen and starving.

Gathering him up in his arms, the abandoned boy
carried the poor dog to his fire where first he warmed
him next to his own bare skin. For some time Pakilawa
sat there in front of his blazing fire, embracing the
small animal. . . crooning to him, "Nitaya . . .
Nitayiitha . . . Nitaya"--Oh! My pet . . . My little
pet . . . My pet.

The shivering **wi?shi** listen to these fond words as long as he could stand them. When he had warmed a little he said . . . to himself, not speaking so that Pakilawa could hear him, "**Nimaachiwa**--Small in body I am. That much is true, but this lad's **tayiitha** I am not. I am nobody's little pet! This bare, naked hairless fellow does not understand who I am. He doesn't even understand I am his **Hopawaaka**--his Spirit Guardian, when here I am sitting in his lap."

When the small **wi?shi** had warmed enough that his jaws no longer clattered together, when he became comfortable enough to compose himself, he looked up at Thrown Away and spoke, this time aloud so the boy could hear him.

"**Haa!** N?thiimetha," he said, "Listen to me my Younger Brother! Listen! Hereafter, I will keep you company. I will be your compnion. I will talk to you so you will not be lonely. And from time to time I will give you advice; I will instruct you. First thing to do--we must find the snuggest lodge in the village for our home, for we have no bear robes or beaver pelts to cover and warm us, while I have only scanty fur and you . . . look at you, you have almost none at all. Then Younger Brother we will go and scour the village and fields to gather in all the corn we can find. Next we must find an old bow and some arrows in one of the wiikiwaki. With this warm fire, and the snug lodge, and the bow, and the corn we can survive the Frozen Days.

Thrown Away obeyed his new found brother's direction. He did not expect to find much, but after a diligent search he was pleased to locate a large amount of forgotten corn and an old bow with some not-quite-straight arrows. In another longhouse he even found some feathers to fletch the arrows that they would fly true. With his new weapons during the coming weeks the boy often killed small birds and squirrels. These he shared most carefully with the dog, his elder-brother. In this fashion they lived comfortably through the Frozen Days.

Shkipiyekiishthewa--The-Days-When-There-Is-Sap-In-The-Trees came and went. **Hotehiminikiishthwa**--The-Days-Of-Ripe-Strawberries passed, as well. And when the blackberries had ripened, been collected, and eaten Pakilawa remembered it was time to plant **taami**--corn. So in these warm days Thrown Away and Brother-

Dog carefully sowed their few remaining grains of **taami** in small hills of dirt. Brother-Dog for his share helped by scratching out the holes for the corn-seeds.

After the hot days ended, in **Tawakikiisheki** when the leaves turned red and the first frosts came, the boy and the dog gathered in a good harvest. It was then that Brother Dog again instructed Throw Away. "Now, my younger brother," he said, "I think we must try to find our friends and kinfolk, those who abandoned us here! No doubt they believed we would freeze and starve, but we must try to locate where they are."

"You are now large and strong enough to kill deer," Elder Brother-Dog continued, "but I am puny, scrawny, and ugly. If we can get some venison to eat, my appearance will soon much improve, and so even will your own. Our friends are not far distant from us now, and I know the journey will not be a long one."

Pakilawa agreed readily. He fastened on Brother-Dog's back a pack of corn, taking another pack for himself to carry, together with his bow and arrows and a flint knife he had found in a lodge. Thus equipped they set out on their trip.

After traveling all the first day they made camp. Long after the sun traveled beneath the rim of the Island, near midnight, Brother-Dog wakened from a deep sleep and called out, "My younger brother are you asleep still?"

Thrown Away tossed, rolled-over, wakened, and replied, "No, not now. What is it?"

"I have important news to tell you," answered Dog-Brother. "It is **niwiiishika?powe**--I have dreamed a strong dream. I think good fortune awaits us nearby for I have dreamed of Bear. And now that I am awake I can smell **m?kwa** nearby. But we will give this bear peace and let him sleep the rest of the night. Then just before first light we will go and find him. He will be hard to kill, such a great **m?kwa** is he, but together we can do it if we take care. We will slay him by approaching him closely before we attack. You will fire one of your arrows into him, and then I will seize him by the hind legs and hold him tightly. You will then fire three more arrows into him and thus, together, we shall kill him."

In the morning, just before Sun appeared, the travelers set out again. At the time and the place dreamed by Brother-Dog they came within sight of a huge black bear. They crept silently toward him. When they were very close, Thrown Away rose and fired an arrow square into the bear's chest, whereupon Brother-Dog seized him tightly by the hind legs and the young man loosed three more arrows into the bear's vitals. By carefully following the plan Brother-Dog proposed at midnight they quickly killed mʔkwa very dead.

Thrown Away and Brother-Dog now remained at the Place-Of-The-Bear-Killing for many days, feasting on the rich and savory flesh. The growing lad cleaned and dressed the pelt, taking special care to rub some of bear's fat on Brother-Dog. Brother-Dog returned the favor by licking the young man all over his body. Brother-Dog's fur had gotten scanty and patchy that winter because of their poverty and their poor diet, but soon his hair began to thicken and he grew fat, sleek, and healthy. When the bear's meat was all eaten, they resumed their journey.

On the next day they again had good fortune. Coming across a large **hayaape**--a large buck they again cooperated and soon killed him. Here they stayed two more days to feast on the venison, while the young man dressed the deer skin. Packing this up with the remains of the venison, he placed it on his Elder-Brother's back and they continued their trip.

Soon they arrived at the camp-grounds where their friends had wintered after abandoning them. There Brother-Dog proposed he leave **Pakilawa** to go scout the village, which they thought nearby. The next morning Brother-Dog cleansed himself by rolling in the leaves and Thrown Away complimented him on the great improvement in his appearance. Brother-Dog now left for the **hoteewe**, returning before dusk to report what he had found.

"My Younger-Brother," said he, "I have indeed been to the village. It is close at hand and there I found all our relations, your's and mine. I saw a great many fat, handsome dogs, but they were not entirely happy to see me. Every one that came growling and snapping at me I gave a good nip and threw down on the ground. Tomorrow we both will set out for the village but will stop first on its edge, at the lodge of an old woman. There you will live as her grandson.

Now, it may be your friends and cousins will suspect just who you are and they may come to visit with you. But I beg you not to speak to them or to shake their hands. For you must remember, when they thought you a poor boy--just another hungry mouth, they asked and gave you no help. Indeed, they abandoned you to starve and freeze. But there is one exception. If your youngest sister comes to you, treat her better than the others. Welcome her warmly for she took pity on you. But you must not shake hands with her or anyone else."

After Sun had risen from beyond the Island's rim the travelers set out. They had not gone far before they came to a fine, large hunting ground. There, working together as brothers, they killed a great many bears, deer and turkeys. Only then did they proceed to the wiikiwa of the old woman. Before they arrived, Brother-Dog cautioned Pakilawa. "I will never speak to you in the presence of others," he warned. "You must not betray my secret, my hidden power, for I must not be known for what I am."

When they arrived at the old woman's home she welcomed the mayokiileni--this strange young man and asked whence he had come. As they talked she became increasingly suspicious about his origins and true identity. Thrown Away finally confided in her, telling her his whole story, everything except the special part about Brother-Dog. In the end, he told her he had hunted with just a little success near her lodge and had a little meat for her. This she could have for her own use, he added, if she would send for it.

Old Woman told Thrown Away his father was still hokima of the village and that he would be happy to accept the young man back into his wiikiwa. And it would be proper for the chief himself to send for the game Pakilawa had killed, she suggested. But Thrown Away forbade her to even mention who he truly was. He declared strongly he had no desire even to meet his relatives. But Old Woman prevailed . . . finally Thrown Away agreed she could ask the chief, his father, to send for the meat cached nearby.

42

Next morning, Grandmother went into the village center to the chief's lodge. She told him her own grandson had been out hunting and that he had collected a few bears, deer, and turkeys, much more than old woman could bring home alone. A little help from the chief would be greatly appreciated, she suggested. Calling his people together, the hokima told them of this. Although they thought it strange for a hunter to ask for this kind of help they agreed to go together in a body to where this little bit of meat was hidden. There they could have a good laugh at a young hunter too lazy or weak to carry in his own kill.

After assembling at Old Woman's lodge they set out, with Throw Away in the lead showing the way. All the while the villagers amused themselves by trying to embarrass and shame the mayokiileni--this young stranger, the unrecognized friend and cousin who had grown so they did not yet know him.

Said one, almost laughing, "Lead on mighty hunter! Take us to where you have hidden this great cache of meat!"

Whispered another, just loudly enough for Pakilawa to overhear, "Such perfectly ugly, crooked arrows! Such tattered feathers they are fletched with!"

And another, "Such a puny bow! Such a flimsy bow-string! Such a dull flint knife!"

And yet one more, "This young fellow must truly be a masterful hunter to kill even possums and porcupines with such poor weapons!"

But they had not gone far past Grandmother's wiikiwa before they came in sight of Thrown Away's mountain of deer, bears, and turkeys. Now it was these foolish villagers discovered they were weary of wearing inside out their ma?kithene--their moccasins. Never had any of the villagers seen such vast piles of meat; and so they stayed silent with their surprise. But they also got suspicious. "Who was this young stranger," one elder finally asked, "who had taken so much game near their village when they had little or no success?"

"How can that be Old Woman's grandson," inquired another, "for all her grandchildren are long dead as everyone knows?"

But finally they struggled--heavily laden--back to the village, able to carry only half of the meat on the first trip, all of them together. This half Grandmother gave them as a present for their services.

The chief's counsellors then gathered around to discuss these strange events. They asked his opinions, but agreed with none he offered. Finally, one elder suggested a possibility. "Could this stranger be no stranger at all," he asked. "Might he not be your own discarded son, the one thrown away last autumn in the starving time?"

The chief thought about this briefly and finally agreed. After all, he reflected, the tall young hunter did faintly resemble the scrawny boy he had left poor and alone the previous autumn. And so he dispatched the head messenger to question Throw Away--Where did he come from? What was his name? What was his true identity?

When the messenger arrived Pakilawa spoke the truth, in part, for again he told only his side of the story, concealing the special powers of Brother-Dog. Old Woman confirmed his identity, and when the hokima heard who the young stranger truly was he assembled all their kinfolk to announce his discovery. He then called his relations and all the village people together to receive the young man when he arrived from Old Woman's lodge, thinking to himself, "Such a fine hunter he is. What a useful helper he will make me."

But when the chief said, "Mayataakwi--Oh, what a pleasant surprise," trying to welcome his newly found son, Pakilawa would have none of it.

Standing face-to-face with his father, he reminded him that he had been thrown away, deserted, left to starve and die by himself with no one to comfort him. "I have no obligations to you," Thrown Away told his father forcefully. "I will acknowledge none as my relative other than my younger sister, for alone of all of you she risked herself and your displeasure to leave me a little fire. Only my sister will I recognize," said he.

So saying, Pakilawa, who still obeyed his companions's instructions in all ways, had busied himself industriously while they were separate these eight days, hunting game so that Brother-Dog would have much fine venison to feast on when he arrived. Soon thereafter they went out hunting together, as they had in the earlier days.

While on the trail, Brother-Dog told Pakilawa, "Again I have dreamed a strong dream, that some great event is to occur. But I did not see clearly what it was. I must return to the village once more to discover what is to happen that may affect my younger brother."

Brother-Dog went to the village and, after scouting about, returned to report his findings. He had visited each and every lodge, he told Throw Away. No one had paid him any attention because none yet knew of his special power. Thus he had been able to listen in on many conversations--even the chief's council meetings. And he had detected the plans of the villagers. A great number of neenaw?tooki-- warriors had assembled and agreed to go on the warpath. They planned to capture two prisoners and only then to return homeward.

Pakilawa, who had already proved himself to be an uncommon hunter, was greatly pleased at this news. He informed Brother-Dog of his strong wish to accompany the warriors, since he had never before taken the war-trail, but he asked his Elder Brother's advice and his consent. Brother-Dog advised him that he should indeed go, adding that he would accompany him to help. So they returned to the village where Thrown Away offered his services, which were gladly accepted by the Neenaw?tooma--the Chief-Of-The-Warriors. So it was that Thrown Away set out with the warriors, who were amused to see him accompanied by his sleek and faithful dog, an unusual sight.

After traveling together for four days, Brother-Dog politely took his leave of Pakilawa. But before parting he again instructed his younger-brother. "The next day you will make a feast of bear's flesh," he commanded. "But if your companions cannot eat all the bear-meat," he continued, "you will immediately sit down and eat every remaining morsel of it by yourself, no matter how much remains."

45

On the next morning **Pakilawa** sent out two young hunters, who soon returned with a great fat bear. This carcass he had dressed and roasted until it was done to a turn. Meanwhile, he adorned himself with black paint on his face and arms and body. He ornamented his head with eagle feathers. He hung around his neck the skin and feathers of a crow. And then he sang his war song. Only then did he permit the assembled **neenaw?tooki** to eat. After they had eaten every bite they could stuff in their mouths, there remained still a large quantity of savory meat, far to much for any one man.

It was now that Thrown Away sat down. Praying silently to Brother-Dog for aid, he himself began eating the large heap of bear-meat that remained after all the warriors had gorged themselves. His call to Brother-Dog was answered in an unexpected way, for Brother-Dog sent to Thrown Away his own cousins, a pack of silent, hungry, invisible wolves.

Not seen by any but **Pakilawa**, these ravenous assistants squatted close around the young hunter-warrior, smacking their lips and clacking their fangs as they gobbled down every last morsel of the tasty flesh, leaving behind only the smell. The other warriors, laying about clutching their stuffed stomachs, were fully amazed and astonished to see the pile of bear chops and cutlets disappear so rapidly. Never before had they seen such a prodigious eater as Thrown Away.

After Sun reappeared from beyond our Island's edge the warriors resumed their march. Near the time when the Sun would fall they realized they were close to the enemy village, the one they planned to attack. Now **Pakilawa** told them he would go forward and scout the village alone. When he reached the enemy place that night he found all the villagers asleep and no one on guard. And so, taking great care, he crept silently into each and every lodge, stepped over every sleeping body . . . stole from all the bows their strings and from all the arrows their flint tips. He gathered up also all the warclubs and knives. Only then, laden with all this booty, did he return to his own camp.

There he reported his success: that same night his companions set out to attack the enemy. They reached their target just before early light--they were quick and they were successful, easily over-powering their unsuspecting and unarmed enemies.

So charmed with Pakilawa's great skill in battle was the Chief-Of-The-Warriors that he handed over his own authority to the young man. Now Thrown Away was to manage the warriors in his place. Thereupon they returned to their own village, with Pakilawa taking the lead as they entered, the warriors chanting their victory song, singing of their new leader's great courage and ability.

Upon arriving they found the old chief, Paki-lawa's father, greatly saddened. He had been grieving about his sons rejection of him from the day Thrown Away had first returned to his village. He had decided that there was nothing for him to do but give up his office. No longer could he be a proper hokima if even his own youngest would not recognize or res-pect him. Nothing would satisfy him at all but to surrender his place to Thrown Away. Only in this way might he pay back for his great crime.

When they heard this all the villagers, led by the returning warriors, began clamoring for Pakilawa to accept. They would have only him as their village chief--in charge of all things having to do with peace; and they would have only him as their war-chief, in charge of all things having to do with battle. Thrown Away reluctantly accepted these great honors, as it was an uncommon thing for one man to hold both offices. For some years he lived reasonably content with his double burden of responsibilities.

But at last Pakilawa grew weary of this type of life. Finally he assembled all his people and only then did he tell the whole truth about himself. Now he finally revealed the secret of Brother-Dog, of his faithful service, of his good advice, of his valuable directions. Thanking his people he turned to Brother-Dog and made one last request of him. "I would like to join you in a form like your own, Elder Brother," he pleaded. "Lend me your special power one last time. Select for me the shape I will take."

Brother-Dog happily agreed . . . remembering the days when they had cooperated together, he had sorely missed the company of his younger brother while he was busy as both village chief and war chief. And suddenly Thrown Away was no more. In his place stood a lean youthful Mwha--and Wolf he remained thereafter.

His people, despairing they would ever again have a chief such as Thrown Away, now for the first time also prayed as had he to Brother-Dog, and so all were transformed, some becoming bears, some deer, some turkeys, some beavers, and so on and on.

Nimechto!

--There is no more!

HATOWALENI

The Toadstool Man

Haa! Katawpi!

--Listen!   Here is one last tale!

A great many years ago there lived all alone in
one much-patched little wiikiwa two old bachelors--two
waapinwaki. These grizzled old fellows did not live a
good life. Neither had ever been able to find himself
a wife. They had no children. They had no daughters-
in-law. They had no grand-children. They were, of
course, very poor.

These two gray-heads, lacking all else, were
full of pride. Each one was watchful and jealous of
his rights and privileges in this leaky, worn-out
lodge. They were always squabbling over what was
whose, which belonged where, or when I could and why
he couldn't. Now both were pinched for everything,
but one was just a little wealthier than the other.
He had a small scrap of garden from which he scratched
a few bags of taami before the frosts came. This
modest harvest he would carefully grind up to make
wiipeemi--cornmeal. And every morning he would take
out a meager half gourdfull of wiipeemi, stir it into
a kettle of boiling water, and cook himself a bowl of
thin corn mush for his one daily meal.

But the other waapinwa was truly poor. He had
no garden at all, no taami, no wiipeemi, not even a
kettle he could call his own to cook it in. And try
as he might, he could not get his withered companion
to share even a scanty spoonful of his hot, slushy,
corn-meal mush. To keep from starving entirely, the
second old bachelor had to scour around outside the
wiikiwa for anything that looked eatable. But he
never found much worth tasting or chewing. Sometimes
he discovered a few small bunches of those chalky,
spongy, mucky things that sprouted up overnight on the
tops of old dead walnut tree stumps. These disgusting
things the Shaawanawa call chiipayichi--White Ghost
dung! When he could find some chiipayichi the old man

49

would bite off a piece and swallow it whole--not with delight, but he swallowed so hungry was he.

More often, when he searched carefully around in a wet marshy place the gray-head would come on small clumps of **hatowaki**--toadstools. These he would toast on a stick over the fire and eat, not with much relish, but they were a little better than **chiipay-ichi**. At least he did not have to think about the **chiipaki**--the White Ghosts who had dropped them the night before.

Now you will understand the Eater-Of-Toad-stools--**Hatowaleni** was not fully pleased with his lot. His **wiikiwa** was neither dry nor warm! His fellow bachelor was not the best friend he could imagine--every day, if he was lucky, he had to squat on his side of the fire nibbling on a scorched **hatowa** while the other sat opposite slurping down hot corn mush! He had no kettle of his own! He was lonely! And he was hungry! Oh! How hungry he was!

One night it was very bad. For days the Toad-stool Man had found not a single **hatowa**, not even a morsel of **chiipayichi** he might swallow. Opposite the fire sat his good old friend, a contented look on his face, an empty bowl in front of him. His stomach grumbling, the Toadstool Man spoke to himself saying, "You know, I don't think this is much of a life."

"That's true," he agreed with himself, "but what are you going to do about it?"

"I'm not sure," he replied, "but one thing I'm certain of."

"What's that?"

"**Niwiitapene**--I'm starving!"

"You and me both! But what will you do? What can we do?"

"I don't know about you, but I'm certain there's no future here, so I'm leaving. There has to be a better life someplace else."

With his mind made up, the Toadstool-Eater bundled himself up and slept restlessly through the night.

50

The next morning at **sheepaawi**--just before first light, **Hatowaleni** arose and stuffed what little he possessed in his pack--he was not heavily laden. He then set off walking toward the place where Sun appears. As he trudged along, when he spied a bunch of **chiipayichi** or a clump of **hatowaki** sprouting alongside the trail, he gathered them up and crammed them into his bag, thinking these he would need for his grub until he could find a decent meal.

After walking most of the day, the Toadstool Man suddenly came on a cleared place. In its center was a uncommonly large, prosperous looking **wiikiwa**. It was a well-made, tight looking, dry seeming longhouse, and nearby were nicely-tended gardens. Looking about carefully he saw no one near. Listening cautiously he heard nothing but Wind brushing through the dry leaves. Sniffing the air suspiciously his alert nose at first smelled nothing--then he had it! There, from the **wiikiwa**--drifting towards him was a tempting fragrance, a delectable perfume, a tasty scent he had not sniffed for many a frozen season.

Hatowaleni forgot his caution and trotted up to the door of the **wiikiwa**. His stomach groaning he peered inside--there was no one! There were--he counted them--four . . . No! A full dozen sleeping platforms were built along the lengthy walls of the **wiikiwa**! These the Toadstool Man ignored, for in the center was a large smoldering fire-pit! Alongside it were two stout forked poles! Hanging from the crosspole was a great blackened kettle! There bubbling in the kettle was a feast!

Hatowaleni rushed inside, digging into his pack for bowl and spoon. Only much later, seeing that Sun had fallen far away from the Center-Of-The-Sky, could the Toadstool Man bring himself to leave. He lumbered away from the strange **wiikiwa** much heavier than when he first arrived. After stumbling along some ways he made a hasty camp and fell instantly asleep.

Soon after the Toadstool Man left the owners of the longhouse arrived--twelve beautiful young women-- the **Halaakowi?kweki**--the Twelve Sisters, the Star Women. As they strode up to their **wiikiwa** they noticed the foot-prints of a stranger approaching and leaving, but they were not worried someone had been visiting. When they entered they soon realized Stran-

51

ger had been inside uninvited, eating from their kettle, and they were not disturbed by this. But they were shocked to see what the unknown visitor had done with the kettle of savory corn soup they had left simmering for their own dinner. He had eaten his full--that was obvious, that was fine.

The Twelve Sisters did not lack generosity. But this unwelcomed intruder had dumped a foul mess into the kettle, filling it to the brim with stinking **chiipayichi** and vile **hatowaki**, spoiling their dinner.

The Twelve decided the next morning they had best be more cautious. The Sisters agreed they must discover who this thoughtless prowler was, he who spoiled their sweet corn-soup. So as they prepared to leave for the day they left behind the youngest whom they instructed carefully. She must conceal herself nearby and watch vigilantly for the stranger, should he come again.

Soon after her sisters had gone, the youngest of the Twelve heard someone stumbling toward the clearing. There was quiet, and then she spied an ugly, wrinkled gray-head, a large pack on his shoulders, sneaking around in the bushes. She looked on as he crept toward the **wiikiwa**. She observed as he peered around, listened, sniffed the air, and then stepped quickly into the longhouse. She waited patiently but he did not reappear; and soon she began hearing odd sounds, peculiar bouncing, bumping sounds . . . mysterious gruntings and snortings. The beautiful young sentinel herself now . . . quietly . . . cautiously . . . approached the longhouse.

Inside, **Hatowaleni** at first ignored the steaming kettle. He was not quite so starved as he had been the day before. He had other things to do before gorging himself on sweet corn-soup. Prowling about for a moment, he first gave his attention to the twelve neatly made-up bunks, jumping into the one closest to the door.

When the youngest of the Twelve peeked in she was astonished to see the ancient stranger messing around in her very own bed. He was hopping up and down, yammering and yelping. Startled and shocked, the beautiful young woman flinched backwards. But she kept this bouncing gray-head in sight.

As she watched, the Toadstool Man stopped fooling in her bed and bounced into the next where again he hooted and bobbed up-and-down for a bit. From the second bunk he skipped into the third, and from there into the next, and so on until he had cackled and bumped his way across all, messing up every one of the Twelve Sister's beds in turn.

Only then, looking much pleased with himself, did Hatowaleni stomp to the fire-pit and the kettle of corn-soup. As the young sentinel looked on in amazement, the intruder drew out his bowl and ladled up a serving of their soup. Gulping it down, he helped himself to another hot bowl full. Four whole portions of bubbling soup he swilled down . . . then four more . . . and another four . . . twelve big bowls of corn-soup in all. Only then, bloated and swollen, did the Toadstool Man grunt with satisfaction and stop.

Now-- bleary-eyed--he peered around the longhouse, then back at the kettle. Mumbling to himself, "Too empty, too empty . . . Won't do! Won't do!" He lifted his bulging pack and up-ended it over the remains of the savory soup. Again the kettle was full to the brim . . . with slimy **chiipayichi** and nasty **hatowaki!**

When this repulsive old invader prepared to leave, the young woman crept back to her hiding place on the edge of the clearing, careful not to be seen, by now troubled and distressed. Watching him lumber away mumbling to himself, his empty pack slung over his shoulder, she stayed out of sight. Only when she was certain he was gone for good did she enter the **wiikiwa.** There, looking around her, she was saddened. It no longer felt like her home. No more was it safe and comfortable. It was a mess! It stank of filthy molds and fungus! She only glanced into the kettle and was sickened.

When her sisters returned that evening, the youngest told them all that had happened. They could scarcely believe her. They had never heard of such behavior. But the evidence of their eyes and noses convinced them it was all true.

The sentinel--she who with her own eyes had actually witnessed the Toadstool Man's revolting deeds, was certain they could no longer be safe in this place. So concerned was she with the danger she spoke out, advising her sisters strongly they must pack up their belongings and move elsewhere. "That slimy old man is sure to return," she argued. "I'm positive he will be back spilling those messy sprouts of his all over the place, spoiling our soup, fooling around in our bunks, troubling us again! This is all bad enough, but who knows what he will do next?"

The Twelve Sisters could not disagree. They all saw and smelled the trouble that had been. They all recognized the threat that might be. They agreed quickly: they would have to abandon their home and their gardens. They must do so even before Sun reappeared.

Before it was full-light the Twelve packed up what they could carry and departed, never to return to their fine wiikiwa. Soon after leaving they passed a herd of deer. Next they walked by several fat bears, and then many buffalos. Finally they saw a great flock of turkeys on the banks of a beautiful river. This great valley of the Peleewaathipi--the River of the Turkeys, was covered with fine forests of walnut and red oak trees. On its banks many of these great trees leaned far out over the clear, swift river. Selecting the largest walnut tree they could find, the sisters climbed high into its branches, way out over the swirling waters of the Peleewaathipi.

The Toadstool Man had risen early, hoping to catch the owners of this longhouse this time before they left for the day. Wanting to take them by surprise, he ran into the clearing and jumped through the door of the wiikiwa. But Hatowaleni was angered to find them gone. He was vexed to see no kettle of corn-soup waiting for him. He was enraged to realize the bedding was missing. The twelve unknown owners were gone for good!

And so he set out to find their trail. Looking around first one side of the clearing and then the other, he at last spotted their tracks along a path. These he followed closely, his eyes cast down so he would not lose the trail. Because he looked only down and not to any of the other directions--neither to right, nor left, nor ahead, nor behind, nor up--he did not see what the sisters had seen. He saw only a dozen pairs of tracks . . . no deer, no bears, no buffalos, and no turkeys. He would have fallen into the Peleewaathipi so narrow was his view except the

the trail stopped suddenly on its banks and so did he. Where had they gone to?

There was no scrape-marks left by a beached **holakee**--his quarry could not have escaped across the river by canoe, the Toadstool Man recognized. Bent over with his eyes near the ground, he saw the tracks did not take this path . . . they did not go that way. They just stopped. Which way had they gone?

Hatowaleni in desperation crawled astride a fallen log that leaned far out over the river. Still looking only downward, at last he spotted the fugitives. There in the clear pool beneath him were reflected the faces of the twelve beautiful women. "Now! Now! Now! Now! I have you!" he chortled, diving off his log, determined to get his hands on them. This slimy old fool thought these flickering images were the Twelve Sisters themselves.

The Toadstool Man plunged into the river so fast he went straight to the bottom. So rapid was the river he was washed far down stream before he could struggle half-drowned to the surface and, gasping and choking, flounder his way to shore. "Bad aim . . . need better aim," he gargled as he made his dripping way back to the fallen log. This mud spattered meddler was convinced he had just missed his target and the beauties were still waiting for him.

Back to the log he went. Out he crawled and down he dived again--this time taking more careful aim. Again he plunged to the bottom. Again he tumbled downstream. And again he stayed convinced his aim was off, no more. Crawling out on his log once more he was ready to repeat this whole foolishness still a third time when one of the sisters could no longer control her mirth. She started to giggle. As she let go of her branch and clutched at her mouth, she slipped and made a scraping sound.

This slight noise the sodden old gray-head heard. He was just ready to dive off for his third try when he looked up suspiciously and saw sitting on the branches above him twelve beautiful young women. At last his slow damp wits cleared enough for him to understand his error. He had been jumping in the wrong direction!

55

Still determined to get his hands on the Twelve,
he sprang from the fallen log to the ground, then to
the first lower branch of the great walnut tree that
sheltered the Sisters high above. Confident of his
success, the Toadstool Man leaped from the first
branch to an even higher one. Seeing the Sisters
closer to him he vaulted to a third, still higher
branch. Now--the beautiful women were nearly in his
grasp--the over-eager Toadstool Man lunged up at the
fourth branch . . that . . . was . . . . just . . . .
too . . . . . . far . . . . out . . . .
of . . . . his . . . . reach!
Down he came, tumbling through the leaves and bouncing
off the branches, falling with a great crash on the
rocks below.

Much amused at this slimy stranger's stupid
antics, the Twelve Sisters smiled, then laughed. They
were not being polite. Instantly they changed into
twelve little Wood Ducks and flew off flittering and
darting between the Red Oaks and Maples. Even today
you may find their lodges high in the trees.

And what of the disappointed **waapinwa**--this over
ambitious, discourteous, greedy old bachelor? As the
Twelve Sisters, the Star Women--the **Halakowi?kweki**
flew off, he was transformed into the shape of a gray
Mhwa--and forever after, this bruised, battered, and
greatly disappointed old gray-wolf could be found
along the shores of the **Peleewaathipi**, loping back and
forth, howling bitterly, crying out his rage and
failure.

Nimechto

--There is no more, for now!

SHAWNEE PRONUNCIATION

Young people and their elders reading these tales silently and privately may quickly scan past the many Shawnee words and phrasings scattered throughout the text. But if they do so, they ought to least to pause and reflect on a fact: these stories were originally spoken in a language radically different from English.

This language, one of the many in the widespread Algonquian family of North America, differs from English in fundamental ways. It is distinctive in its basic sounds and the ways these sounds are combined to fashion syllables, words, and sentences. It differs even more in its extremely complex grammar from English and other European languages. And the Shawnee language is even different in the basic assumptions it makes about the nature of the universe, of the world (which was an Island in Shawnee thinking), and about the various creatures associated with the Southern People or **Shaawanawa** as those we call Shawnee called themselves.

Nevertheless some, perhaps parents and other teachers wishing to read these tales aloud to young people, may be bold enough to attempt the pronunciation of these words, which sometimes look so odd on the printed page. These intrepid readers should be encouraged, for simply trying to say **Haalakowi** or **Tiiti** aloud will help regain some of the flavor of the original oral narratives.

Moreover, by attempting to pronounce these phrases, readers will be expressing respect for a subtle, complex language and those who spoke and yet speak it. The instructions and suggestions that follow are intended to be helpful in this process. They will help an English speaking narrator get to the point where she or he can develop enough confidence and know-how to pronounce the words more easily. There are three guaranties that go along with these instructions. The first is that if you try, you will certainly learn to speak the phrases well enough that a Shawnee elder would recognize what it is that you are trying to say, and you would be respected for the effort. The second reward will come with the recognition that saying the phrases helps recapture some of the moods and connotations lost in translation.

And the third will be the discovery by readers and listeners alike, that their English vocabulary already contains a fair number of words borrowed from Shawnee and closely related languages. Thus when a narrator says ma?kithene, listeners should easily recognize our borrowed "moccasin." Someone specially interested in animals when hearing **waapiti** will appreciate the source of our scientific name for "elk." Because of its French ending it may be more difficult to associate "Illinois" with the Shawnee word for "man"--hileni, but the connection is there.

And listeners will appreciate the origins of a good many place names. The Great Lakes region is strewn with Manitou Islands, Manitowish rivers, and Manitowoc towns, all coming from words related to the Shawnee **maneto**, which means "supernatural power," "The Creator," and "Snake," as well as other things. Similarly, the several Chillacothes and Piquas in Pennsylvania, Ohio, and Indiana are no more than Americanized versions of important Shawnee town names, **Chalakatha** and **Pekowi**.

A little farther afield would take us, via related languages, to the **Kchikami** (sometimes **Mchigami**) and the **Missithipi**--the Great Lake and the Big River. Reaching out to even more distant places, we would find the Savannah and even the Suwanee rivers, as well as other streams in the Eastern and Southern states which were called after the **Shaawanawa** back in the hard days when "they were constantly moving their villages from place to place."

Fortunately, it is considerably easier for a non-Shawnee speaker to learn to pronounce this language from the printed page than it is for English speakers to learn to read--much less spell, their own language. This is because the alphabet used to write spoken Shawnee is quite rational, economical, and efficient. There are only sixteen basic sounds (phonemes linguists call them) in the language and seventeen letters do nicely in writing and reading them off. The basic sounds include seven soft (or voiceless) consonants, three hard (or voiced) consonants, two semivowels, and four vowels.

SOFT/VOICELESS CONSONANTS: P, T, CH, K, TH, SH, and the unfamiliar "?," also written as H.

Readers should note that CH, TH, and SH, represent just one basic sound each, to save using technical phonetic notations unfamiliar to most. And The H used in such contexts does not mark a separate sound at all, certainly not the H representing an alternative pronunciation of the glottal stop "?."

VOICED CONSONANTS: M, N, and L

SEMI-VOWELS: W and Y

VOWELS: I, O, E, and A

Pronunciation

VOICELESS CONSONANTS

P	as in	Pill	Nipper	Tap
T	as in	Till	Tally	Pat
CH	as in	Chill	Hatching	Witch
	(never like Jill or Edge)		
K	as in	Kill	Picking	Tack
TH	as in	Thigh	Ether	Mouth
	(never like "thy" or the verb "mouth")		
SH	as in	Shill	Wishful	Hash

? and H, representing the glottal stop, are pronounced in two very different ways:

H at the beginning of a syllable, as in Hurry or Hit, and ? in the middle or at the end of a syllable, as in Oh! Oh!.

Although this letter, "?," is unfamiliar to most and the glottal stop is not recognized and written, it is regularly used in English speech. Every time an American says "Oh! Oh!" (expressing "surprise") or "Uh! Uh!" (expressing "no") they use the glottal stop, which is the sound in the middle of these interjections. Readers can learn to pronounce it separately by simply saying "Oh!" or "Uh!" and stopping short. Moreover in some Eastern dialects the ? sound is also frequently heard elsewhere. Thus, although Mid-Westerners drink Pepsi from a bottle (batl), in parts of the Eastern United States the refreshment comes from a ba?l.

VOICED CONSONANTS

M	as in	Mall	Pamela	Ham
N	as in	Nil	Sunny	Pan
L	as in	Lily		Pill

SEMI VOWELS

W	as in	Will		Now
Y	as in	Yet	Bait (Beyt)	Pay

VOWELS

I	as in	Bit (bit)
O	as in	Boat (bowt)
E	as in	Bet (bet)
A	as in	Bottle (batl), Bite (bayt), or Bout (bawt).

A few basic patterns for combining these sounds into Shawnee syllables should be recognized.

Vowels never appear at the beginning of a syllable, but are found in the middle and end.

Voiced consonants never appear at the end of a syllable, but are found in the beginning and middle.

A syllable requires either a single or a double vowel, and may have up to four consonants in a series at the beginning and up to two in series at the end.

All four vowels can be doubled: as ii, ee, aa, and oo. Three of the soft or voiceless consonants appear doubled, kk, shsh, and ??.

These doubled vowels and consonants are spoken separately in careful speech--and the narration of tales requires careful speech.

For English speakers the greatest difficulty in pronouncing Shawnee will be with the unfamiliar clusters of consonants and semi-vowels at the beginning of some words. Mshkwa?thapiya--"belt," is a good example of this. One way of mastering this first sequence of consonants lumped together would be to identify the syllables in this word: **mshkwa?-tha-pi-ya.** But do not get into the habit of stringing out the pronunciation of separate syllables.

Finally, when speaking these phrases, remember there are no "silent letters." Each letter (except the h in **sh, ch,** and **th**) needs to be pronounced. And when you come to an unfamiliar sequence of consonants such as **kkwit** (which means "higher") or **kwkw** (which means "temper") do not slip in a vowel to make it easier on yourself! Do not giggle nervously! Do not clench your teeth! But do hold your **kwkw!**

And above all, when speaking Shawnee, speak softly. For the Shawnee ideal was for a person to have a naturally low voice and you would not wish to give offense.

AUTHOR'S NOTE

There is a common belief that American Indian folklore was handed down unchanging from generation to generation over the centuries. The truth is that mechanical imitation and exact, faithful reproduction were generally neither an ideal nor the rule. Even in the case of sacred origin myths, where ritual exactness was stressed in the act of narration, there was much variation over time. In the instance of folktale traditions such as those from which the stories in **Star Woman** are drawn there was even more variability in content and theme from generation to generation, and from narrator to narrator as well.

Readers--and listeners, must appreciate that for peoples like the Shawnee oral narratives were a finely developed art form. Those **Shaawanawa** who recounted these tales were really performers. Their talents and experiences varied. They each came from somewhat different backgrounds. And they performed before different audiences at different times in different places. While each drew upon long established Shawnee patterns, stock phrasings, and themes, they all creatively molded their narrative performances to fit the special wants of their audiences and the currents of their own particular times.

Therefore, it is vital to identify the narrator and the culture-historical context in which he performed **Star Woman** at the point when these tales were first written down. This is important if we are to begin to understand what these stories meant to the Shawnee at that moment in their tribal experience.

Readers should try to keep this aim clearly separate from that of understanding what these same tales, here retold, may mean to them and their audiences late in the American twentieth century. Certainly, young people may be amused by the antics of the Toadstool Man, although some of their own elders may be moved in different ways by the plight of the lonely old bachelor desperately seeking decent food and human companionship. Young people, again, may easily identify with the brave young Ball as he fights off a terrible threat to his family, seeing him as a heroic figure, or with the abandoned **Pakilawa** as he tries to make his way in a cold and hostile world. But adults will be touched by different themes in the same stories.

Both should understand that tales like these served the Shawnee as a kind of editorial barometer, a sharp, public commentary on the problems of their times. The fact that the same stories, one hundred and sixty years later, may also appeal to people of our very different culture and time tells us only that we share some common concerns and troubles. Truly, the meanings in these tales were both culture or situation specific and as well they reach across the generations to tug at our own sentiments and values. Perhaps we can see that in the early 1820s, when these stories were written down, the Southern People were facing problems like those which disturb us today.

The Shawnee elder who narrated these tales was a man far better known to Thomas Jefferson than to later Americans. The younger brother of the more famous Tecumseh, he had taken the name Tenskwatawa--The Open Door, although he was better known to Presidents Jefferson, Madison, Monroe, and Adams as the Shawnee Prophet.

While his brother Tecumseh served as the mili- tary and political organizer and himself as its reli- gious inspiration and teacher, Tenskwatawa helped to forge an inter-tribal confederacy opposed to American settlement of the Ohio Valley and the Great Lakes region. This confederacy was a major obstacle to American expansion until 1813, when Tecumseh was killed in battle. Soon thereafter, deserted by his Indian and British allies alike, Tenskwatawa went into a long and troubled exile in Canada where he remained until 1826. In these years he made his home near Amherstburg on the east bank of the Detroit River.

When memories of the War of 1812 and the Indian wars faded, American officials developed more toler- ance for Tenskwatawa, who was no longer a threat to the United States. By 1823 he had been befriended by the Indian agent at Detriot, Charles Trowbridge, and it was to this official, that year or the next, that the Prophet narrated these stories.

Trowbridge, who also served as personal secre- tary and researcher for the governor of Michigan Territory, Lewis Cass, had been given the responsibility of learning all he could about the languages and cultures of the Indian tribes in the area. From Tenskwatawa, Trowbridge had gotten a lengthy account of Shawnee customs, religion, and social life.

We have to imagine the setting for these interviews, and interviews they were, for the Indian Agent worked from a long, detailed, prearranged schedule of questions. They took place in the simple frame building that served as Governor Cass's offices. In one room therein we would find Tenskwatawa, accompanied by several companions, seated on his blanket on the floor. Nearby, at one of the old-fashioned stand-up desks, was the young Charles Trowbridge, his list of questions before him, a quill pen in his hand. Seated alongside, sometimes, was Governor Cass, listening as Trowbridge put the questions one by one: Can a Shawnee man have more than one wife at a time? Do you believe in a high God? Do the Shawnee eat wolves? And Cass would listen in as well to Tenskwatawa's responses as they were translated by his young companion.

Tenskwatawa spoke little English and Trowbridge no Shawnee at all. Thus whatever they said to one another had to pass back and forth through the mind of an interpreter who spoke both languages. This young man was a nephew, the surviving son of his brother Tecumseh, called **Paakisa**--Crouched. Crouched like a great cat, that is, since he, like his uncle and father, was of the Panther clan.

By the time Trowbridge had worked his way from beginning to end of the questionnaire, Tenskwatawa was apparently fatigued and a little bored with the whole process. Somewhere along the line he evidently decided to try to inform his interviewer of some aspects of Shawnee culture that simply could not be explained with yes-no or short answer responses. And so he decided to provide Trowbridge and Cass with an opportunity for a deeper insight into Shawnee values and beliefs. It was in doing this that he narrated eleven tales, including Star Woman, each of them thick with connotations, symbols, and metaphors. These he selected from a much larger repertoire, any of which he might have told, and those he elected to tell he gave his own special twists and turns.

It is evident from the content and themes in these stories that Tenskwatawa was trying to communicate to the American officials some of the major problems and concerns the Shawnee were facing in 1824. Trowbridge dutifully wrote down the words as they came to him in **Paakisa's** halting English. But there is no evidence that he got the message. Instead he seems to have treated these tales as little more than amusing curiosities, for soon thereafter he put the manuscript in the back of a dresser drawer and there it remained for fifty years. Only after he had retired from a long career as a banker, while sorting through his things, did Trowbridge again come across these documents. He then mailed them to the State Historical Society of Wisconsin and there they have remained until recently.

To begin an understanding of what Tenskwatawa was trying to communicate between the lines of these stories we must better appreciate his own circumstances. A dozen years earlier he had stood tall amidst his fellows as prophet with a compelling vision and a powerful promise of a new life for Indians. American presidents had taken note of him; American generals had maneuvered against him; American communities had feared him; and British ambassadors had come seeking him out with wagon-loads of presents and supplies. But in 1824 he was much reduced from his earlier fame and influence. Indeed, he came to Detroit as an impoverished supplicant, dependent on American charity for his personal future, for the British were no longer being hospitable and he desperately wished to return to live in a Shawnee village in the United States.

No longer a threat or even a man to be reckoned with, Trowbridge obviously viewed him as a quaint toothless symbol of a frontier now passed. He was, to the officials listening to him, little more than a useful source of information about a culture they thought was dying. Clearly, Tenskwatawa and the Shawnee had fallen on very hard times. And if we looked closely at these stories we may better appreciate what they were then thinking and feeling about their problems.

As of 1824 the Shawnee were indeed in serious trouble. Their difficulties were not then of recent origin but stretched back for a century and a half. Until the early 1670s their tribal territory had covered the watershed of the upper Ohio River and its tributaries. But then they became targets for marauding bands of Iroquois from New York. By 1673 the

66

Shawnee's populous towns were ashes, while weeds grew in their large, fertile corn fields. The surviving Shawnee had been driven away, scattering in many directions. Some moved west, temporarily, into Illinois, but most made their way south and east, eventually into the Carolinas and Georgia. Later they began collecting in Western Pennsylvania, and only in the 1730s did they once again start moving back into parts of their old territory.

But by then the Southern People were greatly reduced in numbers, wealth, and power. Their five large town-divisions, once fused into a unitary tribe, were now separated and unorganized. Two-thirds of their clans had died out. And never again could they agree to think and act together cooperatively as one people. So we can see some of the direct historical truth in Tenskwatawa's tales. Indeed there was a time when the Shawnee were constantly moving their villages from place to place, and when they had finally arrived at the eastern rim of their Island--what we call the Atlantic Seaboard.

Like many related societies the Shawnee believed that their world was an Island balanced on the back of a Great Turtle and propped up at its corners by four enormous spirit Snakes. Their Island, all its peoples, the Shawnee proper, all things in it, even the heavens above, the Southern People believed were the work of a creator spirit sometimes called the Finisher. But the Shawnee were unique among related Algonquian peoples in thinking of their Creator as a woman, whom they addressed as our Grandmother or spoke of by her personal name Papoothkwe--Cloud. Papoothkwe, as the Shawnee traditionally spoke of her, was accompanied and aided by her young grandson and a small dog.

That is, the Shawnee Creator was thought of as a woman before and after Tenskwatawa, for part of his new teaching attempted to remake the creator-spirit over into the image of a male. Perhaps this is one of several reasons why most Shawnee refused to follow Tenskwatawa's new teachings, since the majority of those who did accept and follow his prophecies came from other tribes. What was happening, apparently, was that the Shawnee were no longer as secure and prosperous as they had been before the 1670s. Shawnee men had long failed to provide their people the security and the well-being they deserved, and so the role of the Shawnee men was changing, declining in importance relative to the women who had long been vital to the tribal economy and political organization.

In this context Tenskwatawa, himself a dissolute drunken man before his prophetic re-birth, recast the image of the Creator in an effort to enhance the status of males. This novel idea was only part of Tenskwatawa's prophetic package, his "budget of reform," as Thomas Jefferson called it. But the notion never took firm hold among many, and after the Prophet's death the Shawnee quickly reverted to the older traditional conception of a grandmotherly Creator.

However, as readers will note, Grandmother, her Grand-Son, and even Brother-Dog are not absent from the tales Tenskwatawa told. Although much reduced in importance, she appears and reappears in these stories as a protective and important if not an all-powerful figure. Obviously, Tenskwatawa could try to demote, but he could not entirely erase her memory.

In the tale of the Cannibal Monster a sort of reversed, reflected image of Tenskwatawa himself seems to appear. For what was a monstrous cannibal to the Shawnee but a devastating threat to their security, especially to their young men. And Tenskwatawa, himself long blind in one eye, makes his cannibal into a one-eyed devil. Whether he was conscious of it himself, this proud, imperious man--by 1824 a failed and rejected prophet, then seen by most Shawnee as a grave danger to their well-being, seems to have constructed a disguised image of himself, and in doing so made this image the target for retaliation by a brave youth. Tenskwatawa's metaphor seems apparent, and while he foretold his own death, he also forecasted a hopeful future to be advanced by a fresh generation, wielding new weapons with confidence.

The key themes in all these stories turn on critical social problems, family conflicts, abandonment of traditional ways, failures to act wisely, unwillingness to heed councils of the more experienced, and the outright rejection of normal adult roles. In Star Woman an anti-social man forces a mysterious beauty into an unwilling improper marriage and is himself later abandoned. When tested by his Father-In-Law he resorts to trickery, demonstrating he cannot be trusted. We see in the Red-Headed Boy an even more anti-social male who will do anything--even multiple murder, to avoid a responsible relationship with a woman, and he suffers his fate in consequence.

Even in the story of the brave Ball the action turns on a boy's refusal to heed his grand-mother's warnings and he is sore tested in coping with the terrible consequences of his rashness. But he can be successful in conquering this threat only with the help of a spirit-guardian whom he barely recognizes, and then only after Wren is forced to make lengthy speeches to gain his attention.

Thrown Away is an obvious tale of callous abandonment of a small son by his father, a respected chief. Faithful sister alone stands by to provide the spark that first saves him, and the boy can prosper in a cold and hostile world only through the aid of another spirit-helper. Finally, in this Shawnee Dirty-Old-Man tale--or, rather, in its Shawnee phrasing--this Slimy-Old-Man tale, once again we find socially isolated Man. Here this writer had to emphasize these two old bachelors were poor for the benefit of American readers; an old bachelor by traditional Shawnee reckoning was inherently and necessarily impoverished, so important were the economic contributions of Woman in this society. The moral sense of this tale to the Shawnee should be obvious--old men have no business chasing after young girls, messing in their bunks, or fouling their soup kettles.

Much of the symbolism in these tales should be evident in context. But some may remain obscure without being made explicit. The Shawnee did think and speak of their world as an Island. Important events were made to happen in fours or some multiple thereof, eight, say, or twelve. Traveling eastward meant moving in the direction of light, a fresh day, hope and opportunity, while moving to the west symbolized dark, danger, and the unknown. Grandmothers were powerful authority figures, Uncles supposed to be protective guides and advisors, and Fathers generous and kindly. And for a young boy, Elder Sister was to be obeyed, especially when she worked to arrange a proper marriage for him.

The problem was that in 1824, as Tenskwatawa well knew, a great many Shawnee were unwilling or unable to follow these traditional directives or to accept these honored roles and responsibilities.

69

These were times of great and nearly uncontrolled social change, for the Shawnee were caught up in national and technological currents over which they had little control. There were then few Shawnee remaining on their old lands in Ohio. Already most had again been dislodged, this time by the press of American settlements, and had been forced to move far towards where Sun goes, beyond the Mississippi River. Within a few years all remaining Ohio Shawnee were to join their kinsmen on the flat, dry plains.

But that iron canoe? Where on this Island did that iron canoe used by the Cannibal Monster for his get-away come from? Well, as the great psychologist once observed, sometimes an iron canoe is just an iron canoe. Obviously, the Shawnee did not use or make metal watercraft. But Tenskwatawa was familiar with them. Just a few years earlier he had seen the first steam-boat sail by on Lake Erie, the famous **Walk-In-Water**, named in fact after a Wyandot chief who was an old friend of the Prophet's. And for several years he had witnessed iron-ships being riveted together at the new yards in Amherstburg and across the river at Detroit. Here he seems simply to have expropriated an American invention for his own literary purposes.

Readers should not be mislead by the conventional way Tenskwatawa repeatedly ended these tales. The transformation of humans into animals as a tag-end to a story was no more than a standard Shawnee literary device. This is only a means of stopping the action and redirecting the listener's attention back to the present. To stress this point--these are not cute Indian folktales about how Blue Bird got the black streaks under his eyes or why it is that Wolf is always running up and down howling all the time.

No, using conventional plots, symbols, phrasings, and devices, Tenskwatawa was creating a commentary on his people and their condition. These are strongly felt remarks about Shawnee social problems. For this society was in trouble. Many adult men were rejecting marriage, while others abandoned their wives and children entirely. Important leaders deserted or failed their people, boys would not heed their elders, and thoughtless, impetuous people brought many dangers to the community. But there was hope for the Shawnee, the Prophet made clear while recasting these stories for Charles Trowbridge's consideration. Those who did listen to their old spiritual helpers could conquer.

Young men could learn in spite of their errors. New leadership would appear. And throughout, women, old and young, remained a stout link in the Shawnee Great-Chain-Of-Being. The Southern People, in some fashion, using their own resources, would endure. Trowbridge had started the session by questioning the Prophet about a dying Shawnee past; Tenskwatawa ended it by casting images of their troubled present and hoped for future.

SUGGESTED ADDITIONAL READINGS

Callender, Charles

    1978 Shawnee. In, William C. Sturtevant, ed.
    Handbook of North American Indians, Vol.
    15, Northeast, pp. 622-35 (Bruce G.
    Trigger, ed.). Washington: Smithsonian
    Institution.

    There is no good, full-scale, modern history of
the Shawnee. Callender's brief essay is the best
introduction to the history and culture of this society. Moreover, the volume it is in contains many
essays on other related and neighboring societies, as
well as on prehistory, languages, and related topics.
This volume is a best buy for anyone seriously interested in the native peoples of Northeastern North
America.

* * * * *

Clifton, James A.

    1977 The Prairie People: Continuity and Change
    in Potawatomi Indian Culture, 1665-1965.
    Lawrence: Regents Press of Kansas.

    Because of the lack of good lengthy studies of
the Shawnee, one must turn to books about related and
neighboring peoples. The Potawatomi were often closely associated with the Shawnee, and many but not all
were supporters of Tecumsah his brother Tenskwatawa.
See pp. 131-246 for a detailed portrayal of the historical events surrounding the rise and fall of the
Shawnwee Prophet and his Brother.

* * * * *

Drake, Benjamin

> 1841 Life of Tecumseh and His Brother the Prophet. Cincinnati (Reprinted 1969, New York: Arno Press).

Written close in time to the dramatic events of the Prophet's life, this recently reprinted classic is still valuable, although it has numerous biases.

* * * * *

Edmunds, R. David

> 1983 The Shawnee Prophet. Lincoln: University of Nebraska Press.

A good recent biography of Tenskwatawa; not particularly difficult reading. The author was apparently unaware of the Trowbridge manuscripts that the Prophet dictated, hence he missed an opportunity to appreciate his thinking at a critical turning point in his life.

* * * * *

Harvey, Henry

> 1855 History of the Shawnee Indians from the Year 1681-1854. Cincinnati: E. Morgan.

A classic history of the Shawnee, written by a Quaker missionary who had been heavily involved with them in Ohio in his younger days. Not an easy book to find, as it is generally in rare book collections and does not circulate.

* * * * *

Howard, James H.

> 1981 Shawnee! The Ceremonialism of a Native Indian Tribe and Its Cultural Background. Athens: Ohio University Press.

This excellent volume, by an anthropologist who knew the modern Shawnee and their culture-history very well, is a fine study of Shawnee religion and ceremonialism. It was the last major book by the distinguished Professor Howard before his untimely death.

* * * * *

Kinietz, Vernon, and E.W. Voegelin, eds.

1939 Shawnese Traditions; C.C. Trowbridge's Account. Occasional Papers of the Museum of Anthropology. Ann Arbor: University of Michigan.

Here the editors, Kinietz and Voegelin, piece together a view of Shawnee society and culture based upon the interviews Trowbridge obtain in the 1820s from Tenskwatawa and his arch-rival, the pro-American Shawnee chief Black Hoof. Very interesting older study.

* * * * *

Schorer, C.E.

1959 Indian Tales of C.C. Trowbridge: The Toadstool Man. Midwest Folklore 9: 139-43.

1960 Indian Tales of C.C. Trowbridge: The Red Head. Midwest Folklore 10: 86-95.

1962 Indian Tales of C.C. Trowbridge: The Star Woman. Midwest Folklore 12: 17-23.

1964 Indian Tales of C.C. Trowbridge: The Gambler. Midwest Folklore 13: 229-35.

1965 Indian Tales of C.C. Trowbridge: The Man Eater Spirit. Southern Folklore Quarterly 29: 309-318.

1967 Indian Tales of C.C. Trowbridge: The Giants. Southern Folklore Quarterly 31: 236-43.

1969 Indian Tales of C.C. Trowbridge: The Ornamented Head. Southern Folklore Quarterly 33: 317-32.

1970 Indian Tales of C.C. Trowbridge: Thrown Away. Southern Folklore Quarterly 34: 341-52.

1974a Indian Tales of C.C. Trowbridge: The Fisherman. Southern Folklore Quarterly 38: 63-70.

1974b Indian Tales of C.C. Trowbridge: A Story. Southern Folklore Quarterly 38: 233-41.

These brief essays contain exact printed copies of the original Trowbridge-Tenskwatawa manuscripts. Some readers might wish to examine these to see how they have been rewritten or edited for this book. There is a modest amount of analysis of each folktale in these essays, mainly a rather quaint kind of discussion of the "motifs" in each as compared with those found in other areas.

* * * * *

Schutz, Noel W., Jr.

1975 The Study of Shawnee Myth in an Ethnographic and Ethnohistorical Perspective. Ph.D. Dissertation, Indiana University (Ann Arbor: University Microfilms).

This is an excellent doctoral dissertation, a lengthy, detailed, and richly insightful--if sometimes tedious, examination of Shawnee mythology and cosmology. Anyone seriously interested in Shawnee culture and religion can obtain the volume from University Microfilms in Ann Arbor, Michigan for a reasonable cost.